Life In 3D

Merging Dimensions Soul, Spirit & Physical

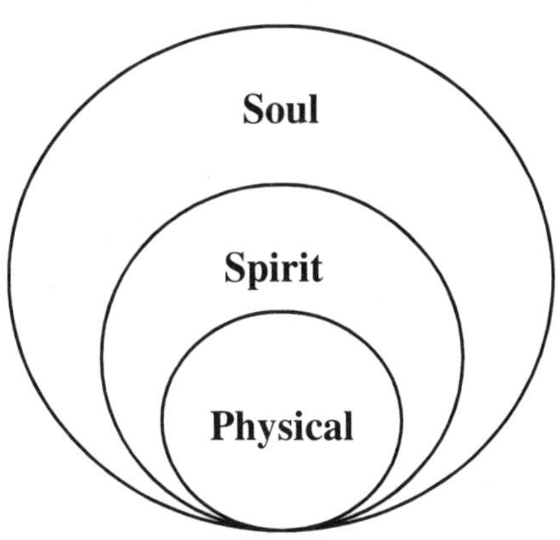

As Received From

The Archangel Raphael

And the Council of Elders

By Betty Rae , B.S., M.Ed.

With questions by Landi B. Mellas C.M.P.

Introduction

"Pieces of the Puzzle"

By Landi B. Mellas

I've always believed there was a divine plan working in my life and the synchronicity of meeting Betty Rae in 2000 proved that. Back in 1991, I had a lucid dream of a strange being with pure white hair surrounding his face like a halo of light. A flame of purple spewed from the top of his head. His crystal blue eyes drew me in so deeply that I was afraid of merging with him and losing my own identity.

A dark-haired man beside this strange being held up a large Persian rug of intricate design. *Have I got a deal for you!* he said telepathically, a coy smile sliding across his face.

"I don't need a rug!" I told him.

The man just smiled broader and continued holding it up for me to see, urging me to focus on this "magic carpet," as if I should jump on it and fly away!

When I awoke, I carefully wrote down my experience—more reality than dream it had seemed to me.

Months later, a psychic artist drew an exact portrait of the first man, white hair, purple flame and all, without any knowledge of my dream beforehand. She informed me that he wished to be called "Alzar." This was confirmation that my dream was indeed a reality, an out-of-body encounter.

After relating this meeting with Alzar, Betty Rae told me how she first met her guides. When she acquired her first computer in the early '80's, she dubbed it SOM (Soul of Me), journaling as though talking to her own soul.

One day a message spilled through her mind and her fingers and onto the computer keyboard. *We are called Hagar and Omar. We have been with you since the beginning of time.*

Betty Rae jerked her hands away, staring at the computer screen. Who was this "voice" that spoke to her? "Are you angels?" she typed.

We are not 'angels' as you know them.

She asked, "How did you get those weird names?"

You gave them to us in a past incarnation in Persia when you could see and hear us, the voice replied.

Twenty years later, during the writing of this book, Hagar revealed his true identity as the Archangel Raphael. This beloved friend gives Betty Rae unconditional love and wisdom that she has shared with others for over fifty years now.

By the fall of 2003, Betty Rae and I had become close friends. When she invited me and a psychic artist to her home, we had no forewarning that another spiritual guide was about to make his dramatic entrance into our lives.

Before the artist began drawing our "spirit guides," Betty Rae suggested that we have a short meditation. During it, I had a vision of myself inside a pyramid where a man dressed in rich garments stood facing me.

I HOTEP! He said in a booming voice. Then the vision faded. No one could find an explanation for this experience and so we let it pass.

The artist began her session by handing Betty Rae a book and instructing her to open it anywhere and read aloud while she sketched the pastel drawing. When Betty Rae came across the name, "Amenhotep," all three of us paused to marvel at the "coincidence."

Later, after we had eaten dinner and were visiting over coffee, Betty Rae agreed to do a psychic reading for us. In a vision, she saw a group of black-robed beings standing at the foot of the table, each with a face of brilliant colored light. The being in the center, whose light was a deep purple, spoke to her in a commanding voice saying that he was the head of my Council of Elders.

This Council had a propensity for showing up in my life at unexpected times. They always appeared as robed beings but Betty Rae didn't know that. We wondered why they had appeared at this particular time for nothing more was said.

Later that evening, after the artist had gone home and while Betty Rae and I visited in the living room, she complained of feeling sleepy. She recalled a pressure on her lids, as if someone or something pushed her eyes closed. At the same time, I noticed her restlessness, as if her feet wanted to move. Rather than laying back in the chair to get more comfortable, her hand reached for the lever on the side of the recliner, lowering the footrest.

Suddenly, a wave of tingling energy whooshed through me, as if I had passed close to a downed electrical wire. This same energy entered into Betty Rae who bounded from her chair and began pacing.

WE ARE HOTEP! boomed a large voice from the small woman. The entity seemed rather pleased about being there as he strutted around the room.

Since I had been in the presence of "channelers" before, I wasn't totally surprised at this sudden appearance of an other-worldly being in the living room. In fact, it was rather funny to see a petite, demure woman with the mannerisms of this strong and authoritative entity. Hotep had a tinge of jovial humor bubbling at the surface. I could only sit back and watch the show.

We re-introduce ourselves, he said. *You both are guided by this Council of Elders that Betty Rae saw as robed beings and for which we are the spokesperson. We appeared to you, Landi, during your meditation. Wasn't it also clever of us to appear on the page of the artist's book?*

"You've got my attention!" I told him.

Hotep went on to say that he and the Council of Elders have been our guiding force while Betty Rae and I are in the physical. We learned that he had been in physical form as Amenhotep I, an Egyptian King whose reign was during the 18th dynasty. He explained that the "Amen" part of his name meant, "So be it." This was how his subjects constantly addressed him. And so, his name became "Amen" Hotep or Amenhotep.

As Hotep moved around the room, he stopped

to marvel at Betty Rae's hand-hooked carpet of intricate design that she had named *Symbols*.

Beautiful work. Yes. Beautiful! This is the creation that we suggested to Omar to have her manifest. Well done!

Betty Rae had related to me how her *Symbols* rug had come to her in a vision in 1992. It had esoteric symbols depicting the Yin Yang, the moon and astrological signs. Having never seen this type of rug hooking before and not being able to find anyone who had, her guides instructed her how to use old wool clothing and burlap to create *Symbols.*

Hotep didn't stay long. I guessed that he was just trying on the energy of the channel. Striding back to the chair, he sat down with a thump.

Well! We shall return! Be at peace. His departure was as abrupt as his arrival.

Slowly, Betty Rae came back to consciousness, apologizing for falling asleep. I informed her that she most certainly had not fallen asleep, at least in the context of her perception of "normal" sleep.

Betty Rae looked confused, while snatches of ideas and pictures crept back into her mind. "It was so weird," she related, "like looking out from a small balcony in the top right-hand corner of my brain."

I explained to her what had transpired. We talked through the night about many otherworldly topics, relating our own paranormal experiences that spanned a collective 100 years.

Being healthy skeptics, Betty Rae and I questioned this new entity's appearance in our lives. We were reassured during subsequent channeling sessions

Merging The Dimensions

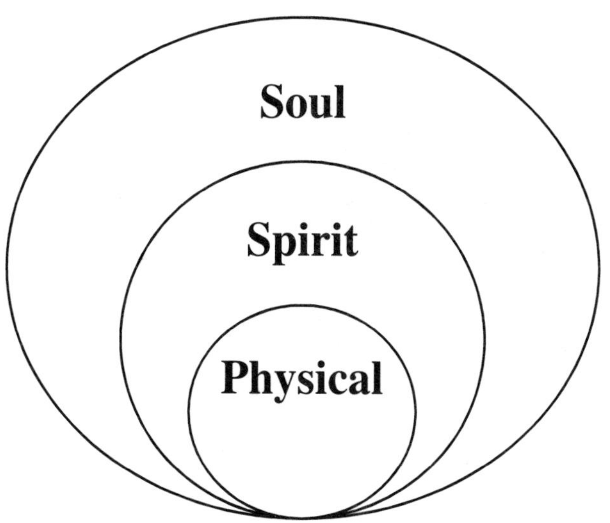

Chapter One

Merging the Dimensions

Physical, Spirit, & Soul

Landi: Raphael, you gave us this title, *Life in 3D*. You said it was about merging three dimensions, the Soul, the Spirit and the Physical. Sounds like we need a manual called "Merging 101."

Raphael: *And, indeed, you have it with this book. This "manual" will show you how to merge your human personality with your spirit and soul selves to become a conscious team working simultaneously on three dimensions. In doing this, you can reach your greatest accomplishment while in the physical world. Since most humans are already very much aware of their physical existence, we will concentrate more on the Spirit and Soul Dimensions for this book. By a conscious merging of* *the three dimensions, you will advance the evolvement of your soul and the evolvement of the human race. Then you can create a better personal world, as well as a better global world. Your ultimate goal is merging with God.*

Landi: Raphael, who or what is God?

Raphael: *God's energy swirls all around you, functioning at all times, on all dimensions and in your life now, with or without your knowledge. It completely rules your created world but can be obscured through the way you perceive it. God holds together every manifested thing in every dimension. The Essence of God is pure vibrating energy. When it manifests life, it spins out energy as seven vibrating colors. All seven of these colored energies are found within your spirit and physical bodies, connected like circuit breakers along your spinal cord. They feed the physical body with God's life-giving energy. Some call these "Chakras," a Sanskrit name meaning "spinning wheels."*

When you raise your energy through meditation and by lifting up your mind and heart to give praise to God, you will be given impressions of these colors. Many begin to see them as they pulsate around the human form. Everything has an aura of color that is God's energy. Nothing exists that is not God.

Landi: Nothing? What about all the evil in our world? Is that God, too?

Raphael: *Yes! The results of creating may look like "evil," but it is still God's loving energy, although unrecognizable in its distorted form. Each soul is a creator in training, using God's pure energy to manifest anything it desires. You do this by becoming aware of the divine Law of Love governing the use of God's energy. There is an accounting for every thing you create. Think of yourself as a apprentice, learning to use the tools of the trade. As such, you must study and master these tools, using them productively to become a craftsman, as many Masters who have gone before you.*

The Law of Love maintains balance within the universe. If your personal world seems out of balance, you have created a distortion of God. Ignore the Law of Love and you will experience the discomfort of your distorted creations. They are not considered "evil." They simply represent the apprentice's efforts as a co-creator with God.

Landi: That's a giant leap to accept that everything is "good," and that we are "creators-in-training."

Raphael: *Do not just accept what we say; prove it for yourself. Remember, "good" is your judgment about the shape of God in any given moment. Everything, as we have said, is still God. You judge it "good" or "evil." We do not. We simply wait for you as a co-creator to see a clearer picture of truth and then begin to create something closer to reality. Your world is an illusion, made up of your thoughts manifesting into your "false reality." Yet, it must seem real for you to practice using the tools of creation, which are the elements of God.*

The Essence of God encompasses those elements or tools that you use for designing each moment of your life. Your toolbox contains all that you need to manifest physical matter. We shall define these elements throughout this book as we discuss the Physical, Spirit and Soul Dimensions.

As you purposefully open to the power of your own divine spirit and soul and to your oneness with God, you create a giant light that shines throughout your world, bringing it peace and harmony. It begins with self, dear ones.

There are three main parts to each person,

all functioning within and reflecting the Law of Love and the Oneness of God. The most obvious part of you is your physical body and mind that dwells in the vibration of dense physical matter. As a human, you learn to create using various elements, such as the positive and negative polarities, time and space and your five physical senses. These elements are sufficient to help you manifest reality within your dimension as you perceive it.

The second part of you, your spirit, adds many more elements, gaining you access beyond time and space. One valuable tool is found in meditation, when you can contact your spirit self. Another is in out-of-body adventures where you can discover other dimensions. And yet another tool is in your dream life. Many discount this direct communication with spirit.

The third and largest part of you, is your soul. In gaining awareness of that aspect of self, you have access to the most powerful elements of all. Your soul has the bigger picture of your life. With the help of God, angels and guides, your soul planned your physical body, selecting the DNA and exact time of birth to give you the body type and personality for this lifetime. Your soul contains great wisdom and knowledge that you can access as valuable tools in the art of creating.

Landi: If our lives are planned by our souls, where does free will come in?

Raphael: *That is a very good question. While the divine plan gives the outline or plot of the story for your life, your free will is the right to choose how you will respond in thought, word and deed to the events of your life. This creates many diverse and wonderful adventures. Your choices make you totally responsible for anything that you create in the physical.*

You are a constant reflection of God's gifts. What you choose to do with the gifts given are, again, your free will. When you merge with your soul, you become a team and will be pleased at the end of your life that you accomplished all that you had planned. You will learn to listen to that deep inner voice of your soul and follow the suggestions given. You will seek to do the very best you can in each moment of each task. When you listen to the wisdom of this higher mind, you can be assured that when you enter the next dimension, that of the spirit, you shall be pleasantly surprised with your life review. But, if you have not listened to that divine wisdom, you may find yourself caught in what we shall call the Between World.

Landi: What is the "Between World?"

Raphael: *The Between World is another dimension of energy that is a higher vibration than the Physical Dimension and yet a lesser vibrating energy than the Spirit Dimension. It is where the spirit body can become trapped between dimensions because of addictions and/or obsessive attachment to the things of the physical world.*

While it is not the "Hell" that some would have you believe, it is a reflection of the disharmony, prejudice, hatred and greed exhibited within the person while in the physical experience. Whatever you believe, focus on and have strong intent to experience, will continue in your afterlife.

Landi: Would you explain what some call the "Astral Body?"

Raphael: *Your spirit body is what some call the "Astral Body." It expresses your emotions, concepts and beliefs of your human existence. It has a faster vibrating energy that takes on a duplicate of your physical form. This spirit body is born with you into the Physical Dimension like a warm blanket tightly wrapped around you. When you sleep, your duplicate body can move freely between di-*

mensions in out-of-body travel and in dreams.

After death, your spirit separates from your physical body and travels into the Spirit Dimension or as some call it, the Astral World, for a time of rest and evaluation before the final transition back to your soul. There is only peace and harmony in this dimension.

The environment of the Spirit Dimension is much less dense than the physical. It is still similar to the physical world in its symbology, being made up of pliable energy that can be used to create whatever your spirit mind can perceive. These manifestations will reflect your knowledge of the elements of creation and will guide you to the precise place within that dimension where like attracts like.

Landi: Is this place what people call "Heaven?"

Raphael: *This faster vibration of the Spirit Dimension is often called "Heaven." It will bring to the spirit all the imagined comforts of such a place. At this point, after death to the physical body, you have lost one player on the team. You are still connected to your soul, for the Spirit Dimension is also an opportunity for learning and growth. Time spent in this dimension is a valuable* *transition from the ensouled life on a physical world back into the Soul Dimension.*

When the Spirit Vacates the Body, It is called "Death."

When the soul has completed its plans for the life in the physical, it calls the spirit back, vacating that physical body. While in the Spirit Dimension, the spirit will still express your unique personality. You and your soul will review the life just lived until all the knowledge and wisdom have been garnered from it.

Then the spirit is brought back within the energy of the soul. It blends your life experiences with all of your soul's previous lifetimes. Just as all of your life experiences can be separated into dates and events within a single lifetime, so, too, have all of the different lifetimes that your soul has experienced become part of your soul. Many people get glimpses of past-life experiences as they become more in touch with their soul.

Landi: How do we know we're really in touch

with a past life?

Raphael: *When you feel it within the depths of your being as truth. For example, when you feel instant recognition in meeting a person for the first time, you likely knew him in a past life.*

Landi: What does the Soul Dimension look like?

Raphael: *The Soul Dimension is a much faster vibrating energy that is far removed from the magnetic pull of the Physical Dimension. The biggest part of you, your soul, resides within this dimension and at the same time within your physical and spirit bodies.*

To the human eye, the soul would look like your Fourth of July sparklers all bunched together in a giant column of tiny lights moving in a special pattern that is its DNA. It has a beautiful sound as well. This pattern and color is how we identify one another. We have no need for names.

There are pockets of energy designed for the dwelling of souls. It is much like your homes on Earth, except there are no walls or divisions as you perceive it. Souls group together according to their training and level of advancement. They study and learn about creating as a group. You would call the souls within these groups "soul mates."

Landi: Soul mates? As in "Life Partners?"

Raphael: *Let us clarify that term. The human being seeks a "soul mate" all of its life, thinking that once found, it will obtain a bliss made in heaven. What you are feeling is the soul's yearning to return home and be with its soul group. It is a rare occasion that one of the soul's group would become a mate while in the physical. This can happen when the soul has taken a "vacation" lifetime, where there will not be many challenges but consequently not much growth. Just as you in the physical life are not allowed many vacations from your job, neither is the soul.*

Landi: How does a soul come into being?

Raphael: *Souls are born through God in clusters of colorful glowing energy that define the soul's personality. They group together until they are weaned from that nourishing energy and can be separated into nurseries, if you will. Older souls attend these nurseries and teach the babies about the ways of soulhood.*

In the mind of God, each of these new souls already has a plan and a purpose for expressing a quality of Itself as the Source. This is why each soul is born through one of the Seven Rays of expressing, as we will explain later.

Another influence upon the soul's personality comes from its placement of birth. The "first-born" in a group has more qualities of leadership and bravery, while the "last-born" soul will exhibit the qualities of passivity. It is very much like a large family. Psychiatrists have books on the subject of placement in the family and so, too, it is with souls in the family of God. Yet, while the human may feel displaced in the family when other children arrive, the soul has no such feelings. It knows that it is loved unconditionally by God and that it is perfectly reflecting that love.

Landi: We are always told to "raise our vibrations." Just what does that mean, Raphael?

Raphael: *This refers to the process of merging with your soul, which is the first step of becoming one with God. That is what all humans are in the process of doing. This is a natural state of evolution.*

Landi: What exactly do you mean by " merging?"

Raphael: *Everything manifested either in the Physical or in the Spirit Dimension is a mass of the energy molecules of God. Beginner souls have a very hard time adjusting to the dense vibration of the physical body and find it difficult to merge with their physical vehicle. More experienced souls learn the subtle ways of communicating with their human counterpart and slowly bring in more and more of their knowledge and wisdom. Through this merging, you learn more about the Oneness and the elements of creation.*

The more you awaken to your soul, the more your soul can enter into your mind and body, freeing up the solid matter. You call it "going with the flow." We call it awakening to the divine Source of Creation—God. The soul's energy expands within you, allowing you to feel freedom from the tension of everyday stress. Even your interactions with other people will be blessed by your merging with your soul energy, although you may not be aware of it at the time.

Landi: What specific things can we do that will help us merge with our soul?

Every exchange of energy,
Even a smile,
Creates a new you.

Raphael: *Every kindness or act of service advances the soul's plan for the life and allows it to enter into your consciousness. And of course, becoming aware of the essence of God will advance you more quickly in that ultimate merging.*

Landi: What about confrontations? Does that diminish the energy of our soul?

Raphael: *Not if you speak your truth and follow the inward advice that your soul presents. Sometimes that means speaking firmly to another of what you will and will not accept as truth for you. Remember that you are one with the person confronting you. With that knowledge, you can release the illusion of separateness. You will honor God within yourself and the other person, choosing love, respect and peace—and you will find it.*

You cannot have contact with anyone, at any time, without exchanging energy. Because energy is always shifting and changing and moving, everyone shifts and changes and moves, never to be the same again. Just as we move our hands through the air, we change the energy in the room.

You see yourself in a solid body. We see you as vibrating colored energy. Everything is fluid energy. Any scientist will tell you that. Look at a leaf through the microscope and you will see a whole world of energy in that one leaf. You would see it glowing with a wonderful colored aura.

Landi: Some say that we can merge our energy with a tree. Is that possible?

Raphael: *It is not only possible but desirable for you to do so. Remember, your energy and the tree's energy are one with God. By merging with the tree, you will expand your awareness of God. Of course, you do not become the tree, you only acquire an expanded awareness of the tree as a living, breathing being. You can actually speak with the tree and learn what it needs to be happy and healthy.*

Landi: How would we recognize someone who has merged with their soul?

Raphael: *There have been many Masters upon your planet who have merged with their soul and*

God. Mastership is a requirement before completing the physical experience. In these coming times of great change upon your planet, many will return to help with your merging. As each entity opens his awareness to the Law of One—Love—he adds that energy of new knowledge to his soul.

Landi: Within the vast dimension of spirits and souls, some speak of a "White Brotherhood" and the "Hierarchy." Will you explain these terms please?

Raphael: *The "White Brotherhood" is the title people have given to those who have reached Mastership. White refers to their white light as they have blended all their colors into the God color. Brotherhood refers to both men and women who are Masters.*

The "Hierarchy" often refers to the order of Archangels, angels, souls and spirits, inferring that some created beings are greater than others. This is not so. Archangels and angels are equal to souls and spirits, because they are all One with God. All Masters who have achieved oneness are God in manifestation. All of these creations, from Archangels to Masters, work with each of you on Earth in your own advancement toward Master-

ship.

Humans are always trying to separate, compare, label, categorize and define everything. They are searching for God but cannot see the One for all of Its parts. There is no higher/lower in the mind of the Creator. Everything is One. Rather, think of souls as being born, acquiring knowledge through various experiences and continually advancing until they are fully aware and in sync with God, the Source.

Landi: As souls progress through the Spirit and Soul Dimensions, do they at some point also become creators of planets, galaxies or universes?

Raphael: *Since God is the Creator of all things; souls who merge with that Source would then also create all things, including planets, galaxies and universes. Just as when you merge with your soul, you create greater things, so, too, will you when you have merged with God. You have no power without the mind of God entering into your creative process.*

In your human form, your soul has taken on the experience of separateness so that it can learn the process of creating in the physical. Each soul, as an extension of God's Mind, is a fragment of the Creator in action. You are co-creators with God.

Landi: That's a very difficult concept while we're in a separate body, in a separate home, in a separate state, in a separate country…

Raphael: *Because your physical mind needs labels and divisions, you have a problem seeing God as one massive ball of energy that sends out smaller balls of that energy to create separate matter.*

All life forms are, in reality, spheres of colorful, vibrating energy. What you consider Archangels and angels are, indeed, spheres of God's vibration that have been assigned specific tasks in evolving Its creations within that Physical Dimension.

To help you understand that all of the parts equal the whole, we will use the pyramid with the "All-Seeing Eye" that is on your dollar bill. It could represent what you call this perceived "Hierarchy." It is like explaining the different parts of God's body.

God, the Creator, is at the top of the pyramid and represents the Oneness of all things. Let us call it the Mind of God, spinning out a multi-

tude of energy that created the physical universes. These universes were then given over to the charge of large souls that we will call Archangels. They are like the right arm of God. They are represented on the first step down from the top of the pyramid. The Archangels maintain these universes and assist in the evolution of the Physical Dimension.

God then created all the life forms on those planets within the Physical Dimension. Represented on the second step down are what you may call angels, representing the left arm of God, we will say. These large souls were put in charge to maintain and advance the development of all life forms.

On the third step down, God created a large mass of energy that became souls who were sent out to explore the Physical Dimension. This extension of energy represents the legs of God.

On the fourth and last step down, those souls co-created with God a large number of humans that became their vehicles of expression in the Physical Dimension. These represent the hands and feet of God.

However, those ensouled beings loved the physical playgrounds so much that they forgot they were on assignment to learn the lessons of creat-

ing. They became trapped in a revolving door that kept them recycling onto the planet and back out again. They forgot the elements of God in creating all things.

Remember, there are many ensouled beings, on a multitude of ensouled planets, within a multitude of universes, within the Physical Dimension.

And so, let us expand on the image of the simple pyramid to include, rather than only four, an infinite number of sides, each with an Archangel and angels guiding the souls and humans in their charge on the steps below. In other words, God has an infinite number of arms, legs, hands and feet.

Landi: Whew! That's rather mind-boggling. You started at the top of the pyramid with Archangels in charge of universes. Then how and where does a beginner soul start to create? Not with universes, I'm sure.

Raphael: *Beginning souls learn to create by practicing how to use the elements of creation, such as focus of purpose and intent, detachment, perfection and balance, to name a few.*

Let us reverse that analogy of the pyramid

to demonstrate the education of newly created souls and their steps of advancement. Souls evolve by experiencing the different dimensions, learning mastery of the elements of creations in each step.

God never ceases to touch souls with inspiration of how to keep replenishing Its masterpieces within the Physical and Spirit Dimensions. With each experience, knowledge gained by the soul adds to its own energy and color, like a flower unfolding. Each lesson advances the soul until it has great authority and power. As each soul expands to encompass more of God, it becomes a Master. These Masters are consciously "One" with the Creator and therefore reflect that One Mind.

As the soul advances in its understanding and use of the elements of creation, it "graduates" from one "classroom" to another. We put these words in quotes because there really are no classrooms, nor is there any graduation. That denotes the possibility of failure or demotion and that is not possible.

There are seven vibrating levels within this home where the soul lives, studies and plays. Within these levels, the soul reviews its many lifetimes within human entities, like an actor discussing his adventures in the roles that he plays on planet Earth's stage. Each life brings advanced knowledge in the art of creating.

These adventures are unending. We give to you only a glimpse of the massive energy parts that encompass the "Body of God." It is like your brain cells that have a particular job to do for your physical body. Each one builds a bridge for the other, bringing about a harmony of movement that is astounding.

Landi: I can begin to understand that we are all one functioning within the body of God but still, I have trouble absorbing it all.

Raphael: *You cannot absorb it all in one lifetime. Be at peace in this knowledge. This is why the soul creates so many lives to learn more and more of the whole system of creating in the physical, to practice using the elements of creation.*

You are not required
To know all things
In one lifetime.

Your life is a reflection of your soul creating through you. If you are not comfortable with what has been created, commune with your soul, asking for guidance on your creative path within the physical.

Landi: You're saying that all souls, as part of the pyramid, are learning right now how to be co-creators with God?

Raphael: *Yes. God created the Archangel souls, to watch over the angel souls, who watch over the souls in training, who create physical vehicles to explore and co-create within planetary systems.*

Landi: To me, it sounds like "The House That Jack Built."

Raphael: *It is rather "The House That God Built." The cycle of incarnations that a soul begins in the Physical Dimension is ongoing for many lifetimes. It will continue until all aspects of the Physical Dimension, with its polarities of positive and negative, have been explored, using the elements of creation. Each experience gains the soul and its human entity better decision-making skills to create a "better" life.*

Even after an entire cycle of many, many lifetimes within one physical world, the soul may choose to begin another cycle on another physical planet, adding to its knowledge of ensoulment within different species within the universe.

Landi: You mean there's life on other planets?

Raphael: *You have experienced these "others" first hand, have you not?*

Landi: Yes, you know that I have had what some call extraterrestrial encounters since I was seven years old. I was being facetious, because many on this planet still don't believe there is sentient life elsewhere in the universe.

Raphael: *We realize that many humans are in denial of this but that is all right. Beginner souls are often in denial of those things which are not yet part of their overall soul awareness.*

Landi: Does every human being have a soul?

Raphael: *Although for some of your human race, it may not seem so, every human does have a soul. Some humans have denied this powerful being of light for so long that it no longer has any influence for good over them. The human may seem dark* *and sad. Yet, the soul remains, because without it, the human body cannot sustain the life-force energy.*

Again we say, dear ones, increase the light of your soul within you and you will light your darkened world.

Landi: Tell us again, Raphael, how to do that.

Raphael: *You do this by listening to that still small voice within that encourages you to be kind, to help others, to bring joy through a gentle touch, an encouraging word or anything that reaches out to another to tell them that they are loved and are not alone. You do this by studying and evoking those elements of creation.*

Landi: If we were to clone humans, would they also be ensouled?

Raphael: *Of course. God is within everything that is created or it would not exist or have life. Cloning is not a new idea. But as with every creation within your world of duality, it can serve as something you might describe as "good" or as something you might find "destructive." More advanced beings on other planets have been cloning* *for a long time. Although the DNA may seem the same, the soul will make it different every time. Just as identical twins may look alike, they are very much individuals because they have different souls.*

We have spoken of three dimensions, the physical, the spirit and the soul. Your physical world is very solid, yet it is vibrating energy that glows with light. The Spirit Dimension is an extension of your world where you gain knowledge by studying your life in a physical vehicle. The soul is always connected to your physical and spirit bodies. With your guides, it encourages and inspires you to follow the Law of Love for the life.

We encourage you to become acquainted with both your spirit and your soul. In so doing, you will merge and become one. This is the divine plan for your life.

We are finished for now. Peace be with you.

Chapter Two

Soul Personalities

The Colors of God

Raphael*: Not all humans are alike as you well know. There are many colored rays within God's energy through which souls are born. They define the soul's personality.*

Therefore, to understand why you and other humans do what you do, you first need to understand how your soul's colored essence is at the core of your personality. It affects your thinking, your desires, your talents and your way of perceiving life.

There are seven colored rays emanating from God as vibrating energy, resonating in sound as well. They are red, orange, yellow, green, blue, indigo and violet. The green ray is the pivotal point between the slower vibrations of red, orange and yellow, while the faster vibrations resonate to blue, indigo and violet. Please note: slower/faster does not denote lesser or greater.

When God sends out energy to create souls through those seven rays, each soul is born with its own unique vibrational pattern or DNA that defines its character. This is how we of the Spirit Dimension know one from another without needing names.

Each ray is overseen by a very large soul within that ray's color within God. We will give that overseer the name of an Archangel for clarity.

The Red Ray Soul
Bravery, Leadership

The ***Archangel Michael*** *is the large soul who oversees the red ray. It has sometimes manifested to humans as a warrior with red garments and symbols of battle. It has a strong personality and when manifesting, humans feel that forceful energy. Souls born through this energy ray are created for leadership and bravery. They learn through doing, through action-oriented kinds of experiences. These souls represent a large percentage of the population of your planet at this time and explain why you have so many wars and* *acts of terrorism.*

Beginner souls within the red ray *most often prefer male bodies and will find themselves in combat because they will follow any leader for any cause. They become mercenaries ready to do battle just for the fun of it. They can be "hit men" because they enjoy the hunt and have little or no sense of morality. They live for their own pleasures and comfort. They are clever strategists and make great terrorists and tyrants. In the beginning lifetimes, this red soul will create many atrocities against others that must be balanced in future lifetimes. This is accomplished through the experience of being the victim of other beginner red souls.*

Intermediate souls within the red ray *will seem more "civilized" in their aggression. They become corporate ladder climbers or the ones who achieve a "hostile takeover" of another company. They will strive to be the Captain of an army or the Chief of Police to lead others. They like anything that gives them authority, control or power. Any uniform brings them pleasure for those reasons. As red souls advance, they will turn their competitive energy into commercial pursuits or sports, seeking to be the best but still not above cheating to do so.*

Advanced souls within the red ray *are currently incarnating more often in female bodies to begin their own balance, as well as that of the planet in this aspect. These souls become the silent CEOs who save their companies from corporate takeover. They can be a leader of a group of people who save a species about to be extinct. They turn their organizational energies toward helping people rather than destroying them. They become aware that they are spiritual beings responsible for their actions toward others. Their organizational abilities at this stage are invaluable to any group because they can see the bigger picture and will seek the highest good for the group rather than their own good. Red souls at this stage will seek peace in the world and lead others to bring it about. Mahatma Gandhi is an example of an advanced soul of this ray.*

The Orange Ray Soul
Mastery, Energy

The Archangel Ameliel *is a master soul who guides those of this ray into the position of world teacher and leader. It rarely manifests in a human likeness but rather shows itself as a spiraling sun image, as its orange energy is brilliant and ener-*

gizing.

There are very few souls created through this ray, for their leadership ability is not needed as much as those in the red ray. They represent only 1% of the population. But like the red souls, they are also energy-filled and action-oriented. The orange energy ray has a slightly faster vibration than the red ray. Their greatest goal is mastery of anything they do or experience.

Beginner souls within the orange ray *are often frustrated leaders without the knowledge or authority to lead and yet, they will have followers. They are natural leaders in whatever or wherever they find themselves. They are not yet mature enough to delegate authority without wanting those under them to obey "just because." They can become tyrants of a country, demanding homage and dues from their subjects. They are most often in male bodies in the beginning stages. They strive for mastery in everything, becoming obsessive/compulsive in their need for perfection.*

Intermediate souls within the orange ray *are often pushed into a leadership role simply by their presence within a group. They tend to know more and always seem to have the answers or at least know where to find them. They become apprentices who out-shine the master. They accept* *responsibility for those in their charge.*

Advanced souls within the orange *ray become the great leaders, gurus or master teachers of their time. They can lead without tyranny and delegate authority for the good of all. They will become leaders for a cause and inspire the multitudes to follow their ideas. Jesus, called the Christ, is an example of an advanced soul of this ray.*

The Yellow Ray Soul
Intelligent, Studious

Archangel Uriel *is often seen in the garb of a large male or female angel with wings. It will often show a book or a scroll to denote its focus on gaining knowledge.*

Souls from this ray are often called the "Brains of the Universe." They love the intellectual pursuits. They represent only about 5% of the population. They gravitate toward libraries, bookstores, science laboratories, research groups and anything that will gain them knowledge. They love knowledge for knowledge sake. Even in the very young stages, they will be more neutral about life, taking in information and recording it without making judgments.

Beginner souls within the yellow ray *will grab at new knowledge and then want to teach it to anyone within listening distance. They will study to learn and then try to figure out how to make money with it or how to become famous because of their "supreme knowledge." They will have little or no patience with those of lesser intellect. Beginner souls in this ray often find themselves outcasts when around the red and orange rays. They are called "Nerds" or "Sissies," because they choose to read or study instead of going out for sports. It is especially hard for these souls when born into a family of action-oriented parents. They can never live up to those expectations and will feel like a failure.*

Intermediate souls within the yellow ray, *although still loving to learn and explore worlds, will work more for the knowledge and the joy of learning than to reach fame through a discovery or to justify their existence. Their great ability to focus on a project brings them the knowledge they wish to discover. They gravitate to science and mathematics for study and research.*

Advanced souls within the yellow ray *will seek knowledge of more universal themes, such as ecology, a cure for cancer or other global needs. They will either share it with one or two people or* *keep it to themselves unless it can serve mankind. Some advanced souls will make a discovery and then give it to another to follow through. Socrates is an example of an advanced soul of this ray.*

The Green Ray Soul
Healing, Service

We, as the ***Archangel Raphael,*** *express loving help and healing through the green ray to souls who incarnate upon the planet Earth. We sometimes manifest as a man wearing an emerald-green robe and wings. Those who hear our voice will think of us as female because of our gentle, caring nature.*

Souls born within this ray exist to serve, to heal, to help other souls. They can also carry the soul color of deep rose to signify service to others. They become the healers, doctors, nurses, caregivers, storekeepers, innkeepers and housekeepers of the world. They represent about 13% of the population.

Beginner souls within the green ray *often end up losing their identity and becoming another's reflection or slave. They get caught up in trying to please another to get appreciation and love. They will sometimes work themselves to* *death and die without anyone caring. Some assume the role of service but resent it because they never have their own needs met. They desire to be honored and recognized for their good work. Others can become manipulative and controlling, almost forcing people to do it their way, thinking they are serving that person's greater good.*

Intermediate souls within the green ray *push others to, "Take this medicine because it's good for you." They gravitate from one product to another in the excitement of finding another cure. They study various alternative kinds of healing and will experiment on others. They will spend a lifetime in service as a doctor or nurse or a housekeeper or waitress. As this soul matures, it will give more and more, with less and less need for appreciation or thanks.*

Advanced souls within the green ray *are silent servers, keeping in the background, asking for no thanks and needing none. Green ray souls will advance through their lessons more quickly than all other soul rays because they thrive on being of service to others. Mother Theresa is an example of an advanced soul of this ray.*

The Blue Ray Soul
Communicators, Clowns

The Archangel Gabriel *is a large soul who is often shown blowing a horn to make an announcement. This represents Gabriel's communication skills, which is one of the lessons souls of this blue ray learn.*

Souls of this ray are sometimes called the "Clowns of the Universe." They love fun and games. They love to express themselves through drama, art, dance, music, writing and teaching. They are the communicators who love to play with words. They represent only about 10% of the population.

Beginner souls within the blue ray *will explain something to you and if you do not get it, they will repeat it again—and again—and again! And if you still do not get it, they will yell at you that you are being "stupid." These souls seek "center stage," always finding ways to be noticed. They are the joke tellers, the minstrels and traveling troubadours of old. They love gossip and will exaggerate the story until it becomes unrecognizable. They love to play; if a project is not fun, they will find a way to get out of it. They can be basically lazy and consequently will take many* *more lifetimes to advance.*

Intermediate souls within the blue ray *will seek to become rich and famous. They are the dramatists, writers of popular novels, radio announcers, television personalities and teachers of language and the arts. They are artists and inventors, always seeking to express themselves and create beauty in their world.*

Advanced souls within the blue ray *love to express beauty and are often very creative in many art forms. They are writers of profound books and spiritual treatises. They share their wisdom in teaching and counseling younger souls. They are movie producers of universal themes such as ecology, morality and justice. They seek justice and peace in the world and will be involved in many charitable causes. Aristotle is an example of an advanced soul of the blue ray.*

The Indigo Soul Ray
Flair, Creativity

The Archangel Sapheriel *is often portrayed in dark blue robes, holding a lyre representing the arts.*

These souls love the dramatic, the flair, the colorful, the bizarre. They will invent new ways to do things, usually out of boredom. They will see things from a wider perspective that might sometimes intimidate others. Their peers often misunderstand them because their indigo energy is vibrating so quickly that others get lost in it. They used to represent only about 2% of the population until recently when more souls from this energy have come to the planet. They now represent about 5%.

Beginner souls within the indigo ray *will find caves or barns to paint or will create new inventions—but they often will not carry it through to completion. They are the inventors and artists who seem unusual and weird to the other soul rays. Their energy is vibrating so quickly that it can confuse and intimidate humans of the red ray and create antagonism. These souls do not like to conform to the rules and as beginners will find themselves locked up in jails and sanitariums. They are often very religious but lack a sense of right or wrong, doing their own thing without concern for the reaction of others.*

Intermediate souls within the indigo ray *become the eccentric inventors and teachers that continue to dance to a different music. They are the entrepreneurs, the exotic dancers and the philanthropists. They will turn to creating new ways* *of doing things, making them more efficient or up-to-date. They will seek to use their skills to teach others but usually give up because the "others" don't understand them.*

Advanced souls within the indigo ray *can be chameleons in that they can look like many other soul rays. They blend easily with others but can be spotted by their unique ideas and thinking. They are good actors and artists and seek the otherworldly viewpoint. They can become reclusive, like hermits or master craftsmen who will teach only a few privileged students. Michelangelo, the artist, is an example of an advanced soul of this ray.*

The Violet Soul Ray
Inspiration, Higher Purpose

The Archangel Emmanuel *is a large soul who expresses the concepts of God. It leads others to think of spirituality rather than physicality. It is often shown in purple robes with a religious symbol in hand.*

The souls of this ray hear celestial music and keep their heads in the heavens listening. They think of spiritual things and have trouble getting their feet planted on the ground. They repre-

sent only about 5% of the population but more advanced souls from this ray are coming in to bring people an awareness of their souls.

***Beginner souls within the purple ray** will seek to save your soul because they have great fear of "God's wrath and judgment." They jump on any soapbox and boom out warnings of "fire and brimstone" and "the end of the world." They will be quite judgmental and critical of other's actions or words. They will join religions with strict dogmas and rules. They will insist that everyone believe as they do, convinced that they are sent from "God" to save the world.*

***Intermediate souls within the purple ray** will become more sophisticated about their soapbox and use radio or television to preach their spiritual beliefs. They become passionate about saving others from anything that will endanger their immortal soul. These passionate souls will find a cause and work with fervor and diligence. They will be concerned with global issues, relating it to the spiritual.*

***Advanced souls within the purple ray** silently go about their work of helping others. They don't seek praise or recognition. They used to be found in cloistered orders and monasteries but more often now are creating their own places of* *worship with small groups among nature's beauty. They will create small communities with the same ideals or beliefs, sharing a garden and working together. They still love to save souls and will speak to individuals about their visions and insights into the "Other Side" and "The Hereafter," but will not push anyone to believe as they do. These souls have learned that each person must follow their own path. They reflect the love and compassion and non-judgment of God. Thomas Aquinus is an example of an advanced soul of this ray.*

Landi: Does a soul ever have more than one color, Raphael?

Raphael: *Yes. They can have an overlay of another color. The color closest to the human body is always the basic soul color and the motivating factor for the personality. The overlay can be the influence of a guiding angel or advanced soul who adds a focus. For example, many souls during the present time have taken on our green ray over their basic color to show their agreement to be of service in the work of awakening people to their spirits and souls. Our green ray increases compassion and healing energy for others. Red ray* *souls may take on our green color to increase their effectiveness within the Physical Dimension by adding compassion and healing to their action-oriented duties. Or, you may be a green soul who will add an overlay of Michael's red ray to give you power and authority to perform your compassionate duties.*

Landi: Does this overlay occur with beginner souls?

Raphael: *Sometimes, when the young soul needs guidance and direction, you might see a faint glow of another color, whereas an advanced soul would have a strong band of color surrounding the soul color. All souls have many guides to help them advance. Beginner souls often need even more to help them through those first precarious stages of learning. They will have many angels surrounding them during a particularly troublesome life.*

Landi: Does every soul have to experience more than one lifetime?

Raphael: *Yes but they can incarnate at their own pace, choosing to learn of the physical vicariously through others.*

Landi: But how do they ever get through their training as Creators if they don't incarnate in physical form?

Raphael: *We did not say that they **never** incarnated. They were simply allowed to wait until they had studied physical manifestation through others before they jumped into the thick energy of the planet.*

Landi: You named seven Archangels. I have heard other names of Archangels. How many are there really?

Raphael: *More than you can count. The Universe is well ordered. You cannot realize the number of soul fragments spun from the spark of God. It is beyond your imagination. Archangels are advanced souls who are the supervisors of universes. The seven mentioned above are only a few who oversee your universe.*

Those of us who speak directly with the human species try to bring very complex ideas into the simplest of terms. The human condition does not often accept what it cannot see, touch, smell, hear or taste or examine under a microscope.

Blessings dear ones. Peace be with you.

What Color is Your Soul?

Red?
Orange?
Yellow?
Green?
Blue?
Indigo?
Violet?

Chapter Three

The Council of Elders

Introducing "Hotep"

Landi: Hotep, do each of us as human beings have a Council of Elders helping us from the Spirit Dimension?

Hotep*:* *Yes, of course! Your Council of Elders is a group of advanced souls who act as your spirit guides while you are manifesting within the Physical Dimension and beyond. They help you evaluate each life experience and guide you through the physical life as you progress.*

Landi: Betty Rae and I have discovered many amazing "coincidences" that brought us together. Was it our Council of Elders that did this?

Hotep: *Yes, your Council was responsible for bringing you and Rae together. Each soul's Council of Elders is responsible for facilitating the life in bringing events and people together at designated times. These "Elders" are highly advanced souls who have finished their cycle of incarnations, usually within the planet of the soul's experience. This gives them first-hand knowledge of the entity's problems and fears. Each Council of Elders has many ensouled beings under their supervision, not just one human entity.*

Landi: Is a soul assigned to a Council when it is birthed on the Soul Dimension?

Hotep: *A soul will not be assigned to a Council until the soul is ready to incarnate on a physical planet. Then it is assigned to a Council of Elders who will watch its progress from the beginning, until the soul graduates from that Council into another one assigned to it.*

Landi: Then we don't have the same Council all the way through?

Hotep: *No. The soul will have many Councils before it has completed its training in the art of cre-*

ating matter.

Each soul has a group of advanced souls who work with it from one stage to another. While a soul remains in the beginning stages of development, it will be assigned to a Council that specializes in that innocent but troublesome stage of growth, shall we say. When it graduates to the intermediate stage, it will be assigned to a Council of Elders that specializes in that stage and so on.

Landi: Why do you call the beginner soul "troublesome?"

Hotep: *When the soul first incarnates, it is like a baby learning to walk. It often stumbles and falls and gets into mischief as it takes those first few incarnations just to get used to the human vehicle.*

Landi: How many Elders are on each soul's council?

Hotep: *Councils are made up of from three to twelve advanced souls who are assigned by God to watch over a group that has approximately one hundred to one thousand ensouled beings within human vehicles. Each planet will have their own assigned Archangels, as well as their own Coun-*

cils of Elders, because each species has its own unique problems and circumstances.

Landi: Does a Council communicate with the human personality or just the soul?

Hotep: *They communicate with both, through various methods. They speak telepathically to souls, plant ideas through dreams to humans, manifest in visions and communicate through a channel such as Rae. Those who have learned to interpret dreams are well on their way to obtaining wisdom. The symbology of dreams can be complex and so many give up trying to unravel the puzzle. We encourage all to pursue this form of communication between the Physical and Spirit Dimensions.*

Souls Communicate Through Thought Projection.

Mostly, these Councils help with the planning of the soul's incarnated life and the facilitation of it as the life progresses. If the soul's human personality gets off track, the Council will meet with the soul to suggest ways to bring their creation back within the divine plan. After the life extension ends, the Council is always available for the life review. They help the spirit personality and the soul gain as much wisdom from the life experience as possible.

Landi: Why the different number of Elders on a council?

Hotep: *It depends upon the soul's purpose in the life as to the number of Elders on the Council. Each has exactly the number of Elders whose vibrations fit the soul's energy patterns. This number can change depending upon the individual soul's needs at a particular time. You are always carefully guided by your Council, angels and Archangels.*

Landi: What if a soul fails all of its classes in this "School of Creation?" Is it expelled and sent home?

Hotep: *No, dear one, that isn't possible, for they already are home within God. That is the kind of judgment that you in the Physical Dimension would make. When a soul is created by God, it is* *given all the elements of creation to succeed. It's only the human personality that judges "success" or "failure." While the soul may feel disappointment when its plan for the life is not followed by its human personality, it must honor the human's gift of free will.*

There is no such thing
As failure
In the Soul Dimension.

Landi: What about a soul that continues to create negative human personalities? Is that soul inherently evil? And if so, would it be destroyed?

Hotep: *You are asking the question, "Can souls die?" And we say to you, dear one, that nothing created by God is ever evil, lost or destroyed. Although material manifestations are born, gradually deteriorate and die, that energy simply goes back to God. Souls are part of the Creator and will always remain so.*

Over many lifetimes within the physical, the soul creates many personalities in both male and female bodies. Each of those experiences remains within that soul's memory banks. The more advanced the soul becomes, the more able it is to reach through the veil that separates the Physical Dimension from the spiritual and communicate with its human personality.

Again we say that it is not possible for souls to be "inherently evil," for there is no such thing as positive/negative polarities within the Soul Dimension. There is only God's energy of love that permeates every soul. Therefore, souls know only love. There are no opposites; there is only good. However, in a soul's training for ensoulment into the physical being, some are more adept than others in reaching through the veil between dimensions to communicate with a human personality. Those souls who have difficulty merging with their human entities can lose control of their human extension of self.

Landi: What would these humans, who refuse to listen to their souls, look like to us?

Hotep: *You might describe these humans as totally self-absorbed, anti-social and in some ways "intrinsically evil," as you define the polarities with "good" being "positive," and "evil" being "negative." These humans, who refuse to listen to their souls, can get so caught up in the planet's* *negative polarity, that they might become murderers, rapists, thieves and so forth. They would seem to have no conscience and indeed, they do not, for they have switched off the guiding light of their souls that are their consciences.*

Landi: In our world, these types of humans often end up in jail. What do you do with the souls who lose control of these humans too often?

Hotep: *Their Council of Elders is always helping the soul regain connection with its human vehicle. It may set up a scenario that might jolt the human back into a realization that he is spirit. For example, he may have a near-death experience or he may end up in prison as a way of turning inward and reconnecting with his soul. Some may even have a vision of an angel that will turn them around. There are many opportunities along the way for the human to move from the pull of the negative into a more productive lifestyle. More and more humans are awakening to their souls again and reaching through the veil into this dimension. This is why we call upon all of you to turn on the lamp of your souls to bring light into the world.*

Landi: When a new soul is created, is it required to pass through any level of the Spirit Dimension before incarnating into the physical?

Hotep: *The answer is no, it does not. Before a new soul enters the physical, the Council helps it plan the life while it's still in the Soul Dimension, which, as we have said, is a much higher frequency domain. The Council discusses with the soul the possibilities of the life. The soul also discusses the coming incarnation with its group when they all come together to study and plan the new incarnational experience. Most all of the group will incarnate together as a support team to one another.*

When the new soul is ready to begin the adventure of life in the Physical Dimension, it will go to the "Viewing Room" where its Council of Elders has already begun the preparations for the human ensoulment. This room has many screens, giving the soul a peek at the future. They're not holographic views as you understand it. These screens allow the soul to step into the scene and become part of the action. It can see and sense, hear and touch. It can even assume a body looking very much like the one that it will wear during the life.

So the new soul steps into the scene as an observer, so to speak. It sees its parents. It observes them interacting with one another. It sees the relatives, the siblings, the friends and all that is going on around it. "Hmm..." it might say. "I don't know about this!"

The first life is very traumatic for the soul. It doesn't really have much say about the impending life because it doesn't know anything. Advanced souls have more choices. In the Viewing Room, they can project into the next lifetime, watching life evolve around their potential parents, seeing their birth and probable events during their teens and adulthood. They may "try on" more than one life scenario, you see. They step in and out...

Landi: But how can they do that? Is that like "Time Traveling."

Hotep: *You forget there really is no time over here as you know it. It's like an author writing an outline of a proposed novel. He might try on several possible scenarios of how the main character's life will evolve. While he does this in his mind, we do this in the Viewing Room. It's much more effective.*

Landi: It sure sounds like it. I'd love to see it.

Hotep: *Oh but you do. When you and other psychics read for people, their guides sometimes open the screen for them to see a glimpse of the life they are counseling—its past, present and possible future events.*

Landi: So after the soul gets a peek at the future life, what happens next?

Hotep: *Then their Council of Elders and other guides go to work. They begin the process of selecting the mathematical equation to form the new physical vehicle.*

Landi: I'm a mathematical equation?

Hotep: *You are that, my dear. Your DNA is one example of a mathematical equation that says precisely who you are, uniquely different from any other. In the world of universal languages, numbers define everything. For example, the number seven defines such things as soul cycles, colors of the spectrum and spirit and soul levels. The universe is made up of mathematical equations that would confound even the greatest mathematician* *in your world. Even God is a mathematical equation.*

Landi: God's equation must go on forever.

Hotep: *You could say that the Source is every mathematical equation rolled into One. Everything, both spiritual and physical, is made up of energy molecules that are equations, as any scientist can tell you.*

It is really quite beautiful to watch your Council work out the intricate details. These include the planetary movements to be set at the precise moment of birth to give the human a personality with assets and challenges. The Council helps the soul outline the life but not as a blueprint that must be followed exactly. Everything is coordinated. Then the soul waits until the fetus is forming and it begins to hover. It sends messages of love to the mother, hoping that there will be messages of love in return. It is not always so, you see.

Landi: Unfortunately, that's true. A lot of babies that are born are not wanted in the first place.

Hotep: *We agree. The passion of the physical*

flesh is an action that begets a reaction that is not always welcomed. But, be assured, these souls now in the flesh are greatly wanted and valued by all in the Spirit Dimension and beyond and most especially by God, who has a special mission in mind for each soul.

Landi: Then what happens next between the soul and the fetus?

Hotep: *The soul goes through all that planning with all that help and once it actually steps into that body, it could all go kaflooey!*

Landi: Kaflooey?

Hotep: *Yes. None of it could work out. Perhaps the mother decided to have an abortion. There goes all the soul's plans.*

Landi: Wouldn't the Council know that the mother didn't want the child?

Hotep: *As we have said: the future has many probabilities and yet nothing is ever solid because you have free will. Yes, the Council would be aware of the mother's thoughts but would hope the* *soul could persuade her to keep the child. It sets up wonderful opportunities for both souls to practice the elements of creation and bring rich experiences through everything. Perhaps an overzealous soul, wanting to incarnate, needed to wait longer but stubbornly insisted to return "Now!" Or perhaps the abortion balanced a previous time when the incarnating soul was then the mother who was not ready to be a mother. Or maybe the woman needed to practice the elements of focus and intent upon a career that was dangled before her. There are hundreds of "reasons" for the choices made that we could describe for that one scenario.*

Landi: Let's move forward and suppose that the mother does want to keep the baby. What happens next?

Hotep: *Even once the soul enters the fetus and the child is born, the emerging human personality can run into difficulties with the parents or the environment or whatever. The soul has many ways of making changes so that its divine mission can move forward.*

Once you are born, you have the planned DNA from your parents to launch your physical vehicle. You have arrived; the life has begun.

Some parents can cause much trouble and disharmony for the new human. Many are born to parents addicted to drugs or alcohol. That is not an accident. The Council set that up for the challenges it would give the newly incarnated being. Even divorce can actually be a blessing for the newly ensouled human. Your Council and guides are experts in working out the divine details to facilitate the soul's plan for the life.

The biggest mistake that most people make is in expecting their parents to supply the unconditional love they had received from God in the Soul Dimension. This is not possible, for parents are only humans after all. Some of these parents may be beginner souls experiencing physical matter. They can become swept up in the confusion or pleasures of the human experience and forget their purpose as co-creators with God, as well as forgetting their purpose as a parent. They disregard their higher mind's admonitions to create good—or as some would say, they have dulled their "conscience." These individuals are like a child who delights in the toys of nursery school and refuses to advance to learn the ABC's. Their education has come to a standstill. But we say to you: there is great patience from their guides, their Council and God.

Perhaps one purpose for an advanced soul coming through the body of a young soul parent is to help that mother advance.

Or, it could be the reverse: a very young soul may be assigned to an old soul parent, who can be loving and attentive, helping it through a difficult lifetime. On the other hand, some advanced souls could be caught up in a "mission" of their own and neglect the child.

The soul's Council gives great attention to plan the life, knowing what challenges, rewards and training the soul could gain from the experience.

In learning the creative process, each soul experiences through its human vehicle's actions and reactions to the life. Every human upon your planet has been sent out from God as a spark of Its energy to create peace and beauty in your world.

The Census
Who will return?

Landi: Will you give me an update on the census that I witnessed in a vision in 1992? I saw my Council carrying a scale of weights and measures and was told they were preparing a census for the hordes of people I saw passing through my living room!

Hotep: *You were given a glimpse of a census that began even before that time and is still ongoing. We carried that symbol of a scale of weights and measures to convey our purpose of the census that would be taken of every soul presently incarnating on the planet.*

It is our duty to help ensouled beings with their lessons within the Physical Dimension. In this "census," each person had to account for every action and deed of the present life within the physical world.

Any ensouled human who cannot resonate with the increased spiritual energy of planet Earth will not be allowed to reincarnate again until they have raised their own vibrations enough to make better choices. If souls create humans who still chose to experience the negative polarity in such things as war, prejudice, addictions or obsession with material gain, with their next incarnation, they will be sent to another planet to complete their cycle of incarnations.

Landi: Another planet? Where? What does it look like?

Hotep: *It looks very much like Earth but in its beginning stages of evolvement.*

Landi: Will the incarnated souls who go to this new planet have bodies like the cave men of old?

Hotep: *No. They will find the new planet looking very much like Earth. You might call it a "parallel universe." The Archangels, angels and God have set it up to continue their training within the Physical Dimension.*

Landi: Then why leave Earth?

Hotep: *Because your planet, Earth, has moved into a more peaceful vibration. It can no long sustain any kind of destructive energy that these young warring souls can create.*

Landi: Is it at all possible for an advanced soul to be extremely negative, bringing that dark power through the beginning stages and into the advanced?

Hotep: *No, that cannot happen. The soul does not get beyond the late beginner or early intermediate soul stage before it must make a choice to* *create good—as the census will determine. Up through that time, the soul may be experiencing the dark side to gain knowledge of it. After that, it has to make a choice. You have been told that the majority of the people on this planet are young souls. In this census, they have had to make a decision about which way they would choose to go before they were allowed to continue their development and their training as creators on planet Earth. The soul of the planet itself has already moved into what you call the intermediate soul stage, you see, and it is not compatible with the beginner's vibration.*

Landi: So you're saying that when these humans pass from this particular lifetime, only those above the beginner soul stage will be allowed to reincarnate again on Earth?

Hotep: *Intermediate soul stage of development is sort of the medium, the turning point, if you will. It depends upon the soul's history. If their history is destructive, they will not be allowed to come back to Earth. If their history is just part of their growth because they are experimenting and learning and if they are choosing more wisely each time, then they will be allowed to come back. But* *they may still be in that beginning stage.*

To those souls who have advanced enough, it is always easier for them to merge with their human vehicles and bring light and beauty into the world. These souls are so much closer to God, that they reflect that loving energy, you see.

Advanced souls
Always choose
To create
Good.

In their early stages of embodiment, the soul will not be allowed to return to Earth if their human vehicles continually choose to gain wealth and power, especially if it means destruction to other humans or the planet itself. These souls will be counseled by the Elders and sent to a newly evolved planet where they will continue their cycle of balancing previous life experiences. Their ensouled creations will experience the consequences of previous choices from Earth but on the new planet.

Landi: Then wars and destructive people will no longer exist on our planet?

Hotep: *Remember, your planet has the duality of positive and negative polarities that bring the soul great knowledge in such an incarnation. But in the future of your planet, there will be a tremendous decline in the kind of negative means of expressing as you now witness. This metamorphosis will likely take fifty to one-hundred years before all those ensouled beings have transited off the planet.*

Landi: Does the soul suffer because of poor choices caused by its physical creation?

Hotep: *Yes, of course. The soul does suffer when it sees that its creation is a run-away human personality. It feels disappointed that its purpose to create beauty and goodness while on the planet has turned to destruction instead. No amount of admonitions or guidance can penetrate a human mind that is determined to create for his or her own power and gain. The soul has to stand by and watch. As we have said before, sometimes the Council of Elders will plan an intervention, such as an "accident," that might perhaps cause a near-death experience. The human spirit will be brought back to the light to see their life review. That will usually shock them into changing the* *mind and reforming their viewpoint on life. At other times, the Council may simply suggest that the soul recall the entity by ending the life before too much destruction has been created.*

Always we remind you that the soul, with its spirit and Council, are not judging the ensouled human. In our dimension, there is no such thing as judgment because there is only God's pure love. We see the struggle of the human entity and feel only love and compassion.

You cannot judge
Any human
From your
Limited viewpoint!

We encourage each of you to practice all the elements of creation but most of all, unconditional love. God's love never judges. Begin with self, to love without judgment, criticism or conditions.

We are Hotep. We are finished for now.

Chapter Four

The Other Side

From Start to Finish

Landi: Why is it that when people speak of the "Other Side," they each have a different story?

Raphael*:* *There are many confusing reports on what you call, "The Other Side." Those who study ancient esoteric literature may use the phrase, "Astral World." We choose to call it the "Spirit Dimension." We come today to bring clarification.*

When death releases the spirit from the physical body, it begins the very first step in the transiting process from physical life, through the life of the spirit and finally back into the soul.

Death comes when the soul has completed

all that it had planned for the life. It will cut the "umbilical cord," also called the "silver cord," and release the life force from the physical vehicle. The spirit body, a duplicate of the physical, will rise up, float above the empty shell and watch for awhile. Then the bright light of its guide or angel will come for the spirit and take it to the next step.

After vacating of the physical form, the spirit will go through the Vortex of Ascension or the second step in transition. This vortex or "tunnel," as some call it, increases the spirit's vibrations, releasing it from the magnetic pull of the planet. Some will experience this as a pleasant sensation of pulling, floating or even swishing movement. Some will hear beautiful music during this process. The Council of Elders will try to make this "trip" as pleasant as possible.

At the end of the energy vortex, the spirit enters into the higher vibrations of the Spirit Dimension where it can meet with its spirit guides and with those who have crossed over successfully.

Without this process, the spirit can become stuck near the earth's magnetism. This was discussed earlier as the "Between World."

Landi: Who or what is this light that people describe at the end of the "tunnel?"

Raphael: *First of all, it is an erroneous thought that this light is anyone in particular. It is simply the third step into the higher vibration of the "other side;" the emanation of light that will become the spirit's glorified body. This "enlightened body" will make it possible to meet with other "light beings." Each spirit is greeted by other entities who have been waiting for the spirit to cross over.*

The light
Of the Other Side
Reflects the spirit's
Glorified body.

Some spirits may meet an angel or a guide or even a religious figure, depending upon the entity's needs. They will see them as bright lights until they have made the transition into light themselves. No one will go through that tunnel gateway without having someone to meet them to explain where they are.

Once in that next dimension, the spirit will continue the transitional process of detaching from the physical environment and adjusting to their new home in spirit. This begins by shedding the fears and physical concepts that may still cling to them. Some will go to a "hospital" that is very much like their earthly one. The spirit will rest and recover from the physical experience, especially if they have experienced a long illness before death. Others may choose a small, comfortable room where they can be alone and "sleep" for a brief time. This deep sleep allows the spirit to let go of the families and connections they have left behind. It is an important step in the detachment process.

When a human clings to the deceased person, the spirit is awakened from the "sleep of healing" and is pulled back to be with the bereaved person left behind. He cannot continue the transition into his new home. While this is not uncommon, it is always difficult for the spirit to adjust.

Some spirits are so jubilant at the release from the pain and debilitation of a long-term illness, that they will be compelled to share that joy with those they have left behind. They will seek humans who act as spirit "telephones" and try to communicate with loved ones on the Physical Dimension. The Council lovingly watches and waits until this need subsides and then helps the spirit adjust to its new life.

Landi: What about those people who do not believe in spirits or a higher power? What happens to them after they die?

Raphael: *Most spirits will be awed at the entrance into light and become instant believers with much catching up to do. However, a few may find themselves in a vast space, which will fit their beliefs, until they are no longer comfortable with that. Then their guides will come and invite them to go into the Spirit Dimension.*

There are no requirements regarding your beliefs for entrance into the Spirit Dimension or a so-called "Heaven." God's radiant light shines on everyone without judgment of any kind. Yet, when the "unbeliever" reviews his life upon the planet, he will often express regret at not having studied the "other side." His curiosity may drive him to learn more. His next lifetime might be steeped in religious vigor and preaching to "save others from hell."

Landi: What is the next step for the spirit?

Raphael: *Although time and space do not exist in the Spirit Dimension, the life review is the next step of transition. It examines every single* *thought, word and deed of the life just completed, plus how that affected those around him. Every experience will be related to how the spirit used the creative elements of God. The spirit, with his soul still invisibly working within him, studies his life and learns about the laws of creation from it. No one judges the life. His Council of Elders might offer suggestions of alternative behavior that could have been taken. Great learning takes place during this review. It continues throughout the spirit's sojourn through the Spirit Dimension.*

Landi: After the life review, can a spirit be sent to that "Between World?"

Raphael: *No. A spirit is never "sent" there. It is always the spirit's choice made from hundreds of previous decisions that formed his life. When those choices are contrary to the elements of God, he breaks those divine laws of creation. The results bring disharmony and confusion. The Between World reflects that. If the spirit finds itself in this world, it will not have had the life review as yet, because it has not passed through the Vortex of Ascension.*

When the spirit leaves the physical body but remains attached to it or to anything left be-

hind, it can become stuck in that Between World.

Landi: Does that spirit then become a ghost?

Raphael: *You may call him that. Some of these spirits remain caught in the vibration just beyond the physical simply out of ignorance of the process of death. The spirit may rise above his dead body and hover there, observing the doctors and nurses scrambling to save his physical vehicle. When the efforts cease, he tries to reach the doctors, pleading that he is "still alive; still there." His panic at not knowing what has happened traps him near the body throughout the funeral and afterward. The spirit hovers over his loved ones, again pleading for them to hear and sense his presence. When the family cannot communicate with him, he becomes disappointed and despondent.*

Most often, at this time, a being of light, appearing as an angel or guide, will encourage the spirit to follow it. And most do. The spirit will enter the tunnel and proceed into the light of the Spirit Dimension.

Landi: Do any of these spirits in the Between World ever refuse to leave?

Raphael: *Yes. Sometimes a confused and frightened spirit may turn away from that invitation, refusing to leave until his loved ones recognize and listen to him. The guide respects his choice and leaves him for the time required to experience that between state.*

Landi: Can spirits be stuck in this "Between World" because they're trying to watch over and protect a loved one still in the physical?

Raphael: *This is a good example of why a spirit can delay his transition into the next dimension.*

Landi: Is there really a "Purgatory" or a "Hell"?

Raphael: *Beliefs can create both, depending upon what the entity perceives as truth.*

Landi: Are they really places of torture and fire as some believe?

Raphael: *Only if someone strongly believes he deserves it. Yet, we say to you: the real torture for some spirits comes from addiction or obsession with things or people still in the physical. They get caught in the Between World, craving addictive* *substances such as alcohol or drugs or a person, place or thing. They may refuse to let go of their wealth and power. They create a form of purgatory or hell, because their cravings are never satisfied. They can see but cannot touch the source of their craving. Those who have substance addictions will attach themselves to physical entities likewise addicted, trying to feel just "one more drink" or "one more high." This is a minor form of what you call "possession."*

These poor souls will haunt barrooms, waiting for a human to become inebriated. This state of addiction creates a crack in the human aura, allowing the addicted spirit of the Between World to attach for a moment in Earth's time. You would see that spirit half in and half out of the human body. Not a pretty sight! Understand, this does not mean that the moderate drinking of alcoholic beverages is harmful. This only applies to those who have become so addicted that they cannot go one day without a drink.

Landi: What about minor addictions, such as coffee or cigarettes?

Raphael: *While an addiction of this sort would not prevent you from crossing over into the Spirit Di-*

mension, you may have to go into isolation for detoxification of caffeine or nicotine.

The energy of the seriously addicted spirits is not vibrating fast enough to even be pulled through the tunnel into the spiritual realms. With that erratic energy, the Vortex of Ascension could destroy them.

So you see, it is a service to allow these addicted spirits to work through their cravings before they are ready to continue their transition into the Spirit Dimension. This is why it is so important to eliminate all addictions while still in the physical.

Addictions are not to be judged as evil. Each soul chooses to experience the power of addiction to the Physical Dimension. The lessons learned are valuable and gain the soul empathy and compassion for those in the future who are so inflicted. Until one has "been there and done that," it can never understand the pain and suffering the individual undergoes.

Landi: What about those who become addicted to drugs that relieve pain?

Raphael: *This form of addiction is to eliminate intolerable pain from an illness. With the help of* *guides after death, the spirit will be taken through the tunnel and will go directly to a hospital in the Spirit Dimension. There they will remove the effects of those drugs remaining in the spirit body. You must remember: what your physical body experiences, so, too, do your spirit and soul bodies. You cannot disconnect them from one another. They are one and the same.*

Beliefs create your worlds
Either in the physical
Or the after life.

Remember, dear ones, each individual is continually creating, using the elements of God. It does not end with the physical life. The afterlife is an extension of the physical. If some entities leave, still clinging to their life and its creations, they will create their own "hell" in the Between World.

Landi: Can suicide cause a person to go to this between state?

Raphael: *Yes, because the spirit immediately regrets that choice once he goes to the other side. And as we have said, some will even create a place* *of torture for themselves if their religion deems that they have created a great "sin." Yet, they are lovingly watched and tended to by their guides and Council. Most are not even aware of this. The "suicide" will isolate himself from all others. Again we remind you, there is no "judgment" as some believe. Rather, there is regret within the spirit and soul, knowing that the experience did not add forward movement, if you will, to their schooling of the creative process. Regardless, they always gain wisdom and the experience would likely not be repeated.*

Again we say: beliefs create your worlds, either in the physical or in the afterlife. Beware of what you believe as truth.

Landi: What belief makes a spirit haunt a house, for example?

Raphael: *In the spirit's last incarnation, some tragedy might have occurred that did not allow her to forgive or to forget. Or she may have become so attached to a house that she refused to leave. When you become aware of such a trapped spirit, ask for her angels and guides to come and take her to her true home in the Light. Most will go gladly, for they did not even know such a "heaven" ex-*

isted. Others may choose to remain in that "Between World."

Landi: Can spirits in the Between World influence us in the physical?

Raphael: *They have no influence unless you allow it or your soul has chosen to experience it. There are manipulative spirits who may have a stake in, shall we say, a fortune that they have left behind. They may "haunt" those who now have control of their money, creating "ghost-like" appearances in their effort to make their wishes known.*

Yes, dear ones, there are those who come from the "other side" who will try to influence you. Most people will not even be aware of them. If you are, simply ignore them and they will go away. Yet, we encourage you to give them your love and to ask us to help them. We will coax them to come to our door of light and pass through. For indeed, they have not completed their transition into the world of light. They have not experienced the "life review." They do not even know of that process, for they know only the world and its pleasures that they left behind.

Landi: Are there really "evil spirits?"

Raphael: *We will say, yes, but only according to your definition of "evil." When a human destroys another's possessions or life, you judge that as "evil." We have just described a few entities who are trapped in the Between World. Yet, we do not label them "evil." They are mostly inexperienced in using the elements of God while they were incarnated. They may be ignorant of the transition into spirit after death. While in the physical they might have continually ignored that voice of conscience, following their own selfish acts, until they had become detached from their souls. It may take some time before they would be reunited with it. Eventually, they shall complete their transition; first into the Spirit Dimension and then into the Soul Dimension.*

Spirits deeply attached to the material world may steadfastly refuse to go to the other side. Bless them and most importantly do not open yourself to fear, for in their negative state they will gain energy from that fear vibration. Continue to bless them, to see them in light and to say prayers of release for them. The soul's spirit personality will progress in God's perfect time. This negative experience will not be wasted.

Landi: Can those spirits, who are still in the Between World, possess a physical body and make the person do evil acts?

Raphael: *Not without the soul's permission. Remember, your soul is your gatekeeper. Nothing happens to you that is not part of the soul's lessons in the art of creating. In studying the negative polarity of your planet, the soul may allow negative spirits to influence and suggest ideas to test your sense of truth and integrity and your strength to resist temptation. It is always your choice whether or not to act upon the suggestion. But spirits cannot possess or force you to comply. Those physical beings who do listen and follow the suggestions from spirits are responsible for their choices—and so is the spirit who suggests it. As the element of balance requires, both must also experience what they have created.*

Any spirit that is not resonating at your frequency would not be allowed to associate with you. Like attracts like. Your pure intention for good is the key ingredient, you see. Therefore, we say to you: watch your thoughts, as this is what creates your reality.

Be at peace in this. Very new souls will dabble with the negative as they learn about the dimensions beyond their physical world. Their fears are the catalyst for such events, for fear begets fear, you see. Yet, to the soul, it is like the scariest ride in your amusement park. Some souls love the thrill of terror as much as you do in watching your "horror" films. They know that when the movie is over, they are still safe and perfectly loved by God.

Landi: What about tyrants like Hitler who wrought such horrible acts of evil?

Raphael: *First of all, dear one, we say to you: no one is responsible for the acts of others. During his regime, Hitler may have been influenced by others who wanted power and believed themselves to be a "superior race," but he was responsible for each decision he personally made. It may take many lifetimes for those souls to rectify their acts of inhumanity. They will create lifetimes of service to others. It is much like your courts now that insist upon community service to pay a debt.*

Landi: Has Hitler's soul paid his debts yet?

Raphael: *Not as yet. Since that time, his soul has created multiple human entities that he has ensouled simultaneously. It has taken a great deal of* *the soul's energy to do this but he is well on track now. In all of these lives, he has experienced service to others, as well as being a victim of racial prejudice as part of his retraining as a creator. Some of his lives have been short lived because of violent deaths. This entity will continue new incarnations on the planet in bodies that will experience the "fruits of his creations." If you were to meet him today, you would find him a philanthropist, giving away his wealth to help others find a cure for a disease he contracted while he was Hitler.*

The Element of Balance Is ongoing For all of creation.

Another example of a tyrant was during Augustus Caesar's rule when the Romans tortured the Christians in the arena of the lions. These cruel acts first begot those souls a like experience as a victim in their next lifetime to balance that which they had wrought.

Indeed, there are many scenarios where their actions propelled whole races into a future experience where they became the victims. This is true of nations as well, for they are the same. The United States is a nation of people who come from the ancient civilization of Atlantis, which misused it technology, bringing about a cataclysmic event of destruction. Had there not been intervention from the higher dimensions, the whole race would have been wiped out. Some escaped to live among the people of Egypt and elsewhere. Your country seems to have passed that crisis period where you could have annihilated yourselves again. Instead, your country is simply reaping what it has sown through lesser traumatic events that involve terrorism from other countries. Remember: everything balances. But also remember, only God can determine what needs balancing. No one can take revenge without someone seeking revenge against him and suffering the consequences of that act as well.

While the United States as a nation is still reaping the consequences of past mistakes, its people are becoming more enlightened. There are enough advanced souls incarnating to bring the country into alignment with higher integrity and peaceful intent so that the future is better secured than before.

We say to you, creating weapons of war is no excuse to go to war or to use them against other smaller warring countries that are working through their own experiences of cause and effect. By interfering, your country or the leaders who choose to interfere are creating future balancing acts.

Landi: What about acts of terrorism? Aren't we right in trying to stop them?

Raphael: *Of course and you are doing so at this moment with the greater vigilance and intelligence reporting. You are also finding that more people are coming into the light of God and reporting those who have evil intent upon another. Those "terrorists" who were involved and perished through those acts of massive destruction of the Twin Towers in New York are presently on the "other side" reviewing their life's work and seeing all aspects of their choices. There is much regret, although their human minds were quite content to commit such an act in the belief that they were heroes for their "cause."*

Beliefs create escape hatches for acts of violence toward others. The bully in the schoolyard will often latch onto a belief that permits him to be destructive in adulthood using that belief as an excuse to bully another. These begin-

ner souls do not know what they do.

In future lifetimes, they will become the victim of future bullies to experience first hand what they have created. Those present-day victims will become the future compassionate healers of the victims and so on.

Landi: What about "black magic?"

Raphael: *When an entity dabbles in "black magic," they are calling in the negative spirits of the Between World. These disembodied humans had created havoc and destruction while on Earth. They will gladly respond to the call of those who desire to seek revenge or gain control over another or create wealth and power at any cost. And in future lifetimes, they must pay the price for it by experiencing same.*

Landi: How many lifetimes before a soul figures it out and "gets it."

Raphael: *As many as it takes to learn the "tools of the trade" or the elements of creation. That also includes the virtues of patience, compassion, honesty, integrity, wisdom, knowledge and unconditional love. These tools teach you how to create* *within the physical manifestations.*

The Physical and Spirit Dimensions are a continuation of the soul's education within that same personality for a designated period, until all that can be learned is accomplished. Then the soul will bring that personality back into its energy and will absorb it.

Landi: What does that mean, "absorb it." Sounds like it swallows and digests it like a fish.

Raphael: *The analogy is similar. When you eat food, it is assimilated and absorbed into your body, becoming part of you. There is no division between you and the fish. When you as a spirit personality are absorbed into your soul, all of your wisdom and knowledge becomes part of your soul. Yet, like a clear memory, you can be re-called, complete and whole, at any time.*

We will leave you with this. Blessings and peace be with you.

The Seven Realms

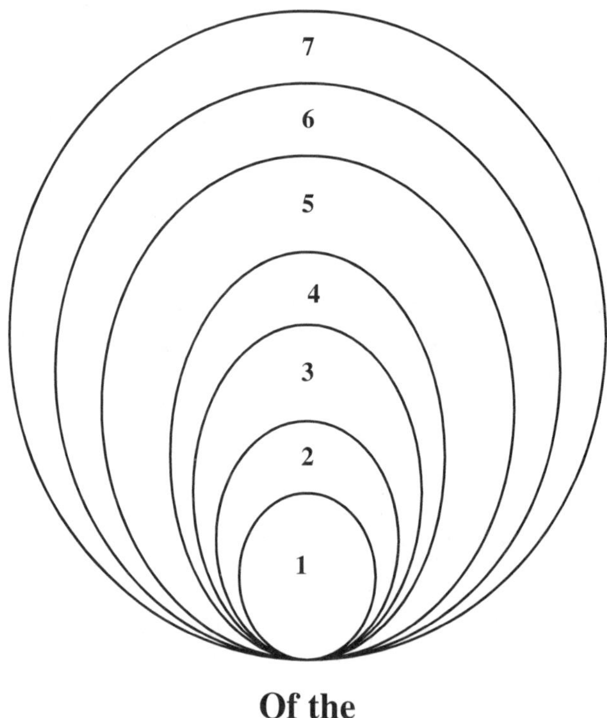

Of the

Spirit Dimension

Chapter Five

The Spirit Dimension

The Seven Realms

Landi: Raphael, will you tell us more about the "other side?"

Raphael: *As in every dimension, there are seven realms of varying frequencies that contain a wide variety of experiences for spirits to explore. Whatever is conceived in the Spirit Dimension is imprinted in the Physical Dimension. This is why we say to you: see only beauty and goodness and you create the same in your world.*

There are so many different scenarios about the transition into the dimension of spirit because each spirit personality will experience it through his belief system. Some people who have had a near-death-experience have written books about the "other side." They speak of it as a "heaven" that may come directly from their religious teachings and holy books. They will create in this dimension beyond the physical whatever they believe to be truth. While in the Physical Dimension, humans had to work through the pull of the polarities with time and space, allowing the human the opportunity to create, stop, evaluate and recreate, if necessary.

In the Spirit Dimension Creating is Instantaneous.

Within each realm there are seven vibrating frequencies, from very slow and dense to the faster frequency which matches the energy of the spirit personality and its perceived needs. A beginning soul's energy vibrates slower and therefore, they will create the comforts they imagine from the Physical Dimension as their experience in the afterlife. As a spirit advances, its energy increases and so does the vibration of its afterlife, reflecting the spirit's thoughts and needs. The frequency vibrations within each realm of the Spirit Dimension reflect those changes in each spirit's development.

Landi: You mentioned different "realms." What are they?

First Spirit Realm
The Focus of Initiation

Raphael: *Let us attempt to put into human terms an overview of those realms within the dimension of spirit. In each of the realms, spirits will create a world that is the idyllic vision of their physical life.*

Beginner souls would create a heaven where they can eat all they want and not get fat; party all night without getting tired; or become the great movie star they always dreamed about.

On the other hand, those who loved competitive sports might be disappointed because the spirit can win every game. The golf ball would be a "hole in one" every time. The entity would soon lose interest and turn to other kinds of social activities.

Those who feel the need to duplicate the physical world would likely be found within the first or second frequency vibrations of any realm within the Spirit Dimension that we will describe.

This first realm initiates the spirit into the world of this dimension and reflects the spirit's comfort zone.

The second frequency within the first realm of the Spirit Dimension might reflect the spirit's advancement through his creation of a cottage in the woods or mountains. This is far away from the first frequency of those who need excitement and entertainment. Each increase in frequency reflects the soul's knowledge and use of the elements of God. But basically, this first realm is a period of rest and recovery from the physical life.

Second Spirit Realm
The Focus of Nature

In the next realm of vibration, those entities who are more interested in Earth's nature will create an abundance of flowers or a vegetable garden.

Some more advanced spirits who gravitate toward this vibration are filled with love for Mother Earth and use their time in the higher frequencies of this realm to find solutions for her problems.

Landi: I visited this particular realm during an out-of-body experience, where a gentle old spirit took me on a tour of a beautiful vegetable garden. It had an even temperature and no destructive insects. Why was I shown that?

Raphael: *This is where you often go, Landi, while out-of-body to study gardening. As you become adept at bringing this Spirit Dimension into your physical experiences, you can manifest it more easily into your physical world. Your mind, with your inner sight of this dimension, can see various solutions to any project you are working on. You try them out in your mind before choosing a solution. Thus your success rate is higher than a beginner soul without this access to the Spirit Dimension.*

Landi: I loved being in that second spirit realm. Why can't we eliminate the physical world and just live in spirit?

Raphael: *Each dimension is a step in the education of souls. Each is valuable and an integral part of the creative process. Spirits on this second realm of the Spirit Dimension will create the future solutions to the ecology of the planet. Experimentation at this level in spirit comes first. Then advanced souls, acting as guides, remind you of these* *ideas. They encourage you in the germination and growth of that idea first in your mind, as to how to manifest it within your Physical Dimension. This is the reason why several people all across the globe can come up with the same idea or solution at the same time.*

Many spirits on this second realm are working in cooperation with humans for the betterment of the physical worlds. Spirits cannot do this on their own. Therefore, it is important for each of you to reach through the veil which separates the dimensions. When you do, it is as though you have become a genius, for you gain access to more than just your five physical senses. Some call this their "sixth sense."

Knowledge of
All Dimensions
Is Part of the divine plan
In the coursework of lessons
For the soul.

Without continual manifestation, the worlds would disintegrate and disappear. The thought forms that bring the molecules of matter together into or-

ganized forms are necessary from all levels of soul development to continue the cycle of living forms. You and all others are given this massive trust—to develop life on your planet and other planets and within all universes. Now you can understand how important it is for your small community of gardeners in spirit to continue their work with you and others to bring health to your planet.

Continual manifestation
In dense matter
Keeps the universe together.

Landi: Can a beginner spirit ever visit the higher vibrating frequencies of the more advanced spirits?

Raphael: *Not without a guide who will help them increase their vibrations to visit other higher frequency levels. Yet, more advanced souls can visit in any vibration with conscious adjustment.*

The reason for the different vibrating frequencies from slow to fast is so that the spirits of advanced souls do not "bump" into the beginners. Each spirit gravitates to the vibration that resonates with their own.

Landi: Sounds like segregation to me. Don't tell me they have spirit bussing from one vibration to the next!

Raphael: *Oh, dear one, of course not!. Do not believe that a slower vibration in the Spirit Dimension is lesser in its importance to the development of the soul. On this second realm, beginner spirits come there just to enjoy the pleasures of nature's beauty, while those of higher vibration come to work out problems within plant life on their planets. Each gravitates to the frequency of their interest. The faster levels of the second realm are for the study of nature.*

So, we say to you: souls of many levels will visit this working realm to begin the manifestations of their work on the denser Physical Dimensions.

Third Spirit Realm
The Focus of Recreation

As we move to the next realm, you will find spirits congregating for socializing and play. Yes, spirits enjoy one another in their glorified bodies before returning to the Soul Dimension. Yet, we say to you again—each spirit will move naturally toward the level of their vibration—they will not meet anyone who is not of like mind or like belief, for that matter. They each have their own "social club," you see.

Landi: What do they call "play" on this third realm of spirit?

Raphael: *"Play" becomes whatever they wish, depending on their interests. The first level in this realm would again imitate the more dense things of Earth. People gather to picnic, swim and play games. Some love water and will create a lake for water sports. They can race, you see, but each will win the race! The second level might swim and enjoy the fish that will enjoy them as well. The third level might dive beneath the surface and breathe underwater to play with the dolphins.*

This third spirit realm teaches true play. It is filled with joy and laughter.

Fourth Spirit Realm
The Focus of Love

In this vibration the soul will experience love in relationships and service to others. This is where the hospital will be found or the practice of many new kinds of medical modalities. This is where scientists will gather to study and perhaps go to the Great Hall of Knowledge to find cures for diseases in the physical worlds.

Higher vibrating entities will come here to invent new forms of healing the problems within their communities and countries. They might invent new means of travel, housing, garbage recycling and the like. In another area, spirits will come to work on political concerns where their countries have dissolved into the destruction of warring parties. They oversee the physical from this realm and send peaceful, healing messages to their counterparts on the planet.

Fifth Spirit Realm
The Focus of Communication

In this realm, you will find those who rejoice in communication with God and with other planetary beings. They are most interested in that: communication. They will search for new methods to bring understanding to the incarnated souls. This realm, with its concentration on the spoken and printed word, is where the ideas for speeches and books will begin. Spirits will work on them first here before they incarnate in another body to make that idea manifested.

This fifth realm is also where spirits will gather who love to converse about subjects dear to their hearts. They will create pubs, you see, where they can sit around a small table and debate for long hours over a cup of coffee or a beer. Yes, they do enjoy their lively conversations. The art of debate begins here. Great minds can be conjured up to join in their debate whenever a point needs to be made. Some would call this the mental plane because the focus is in the mental. The Hall of Knowledge can be found there.

Landi: What and where is this "Hall of Knowledge?"

Raphael: *The Hall of Knowledge is a created building much like a university where spirits gather to study and learn. As with all things, it is really the Mind of God. Guides will present the place of learning as a visual structure. Therefore, people who return from a visit to this realm may describe the Hall of Knowledge differently, depending upon what they choose to study.*

Some spirits may work with masters of any trade or talent and interact with them on a one-on-one basis. Knowledge is available to any of the spirits within any of the realms. Beginner spirits usually have no interest or awareness of the Hall of Knowledge.

Sixth Spirit Realm
The Focus of Projection

Students of this realm learn to project their creations to those of the physical. Artists will project their masterpiece. Musicians will inspire a composer. It is the realm of development of the "sixth sense" of "seeing," or what some call your "third eye."

In this realm you practice the projection of ideas into a human mind through dreams, inspiration, channeling and psychic abilities. Spirit guides study at the seventh vibration of this realm, learning the different methods of thought projection to the physical entities.

In learning the art of projection on any level within this realm, it begins with play at first and then in earnest. For example, in the art of channeling, the spirit learns to enter the physical space without disrupting the molecules of the body. This form of channeling begins first with learning to project into another person's dreams. It is like jumping rope. You wait until the vibra-

tional rhythm is right and you jump in. You try not to disrupt the rhythm of the swinging rope or stop its motion.

Those who have had many lifetimes practicing this art form of channeling bring in advanced knowledge on a particular subject. It is like the one called Beethoven who was a child prodigy. He had many spirit lives within the fifth realm where he studied with the Masters so that he could manifest the joy of music in the world. He also studied in the sixth realm so that those Masters could project ideas and music through him.

Seventh Spirit Realm
The Focus of Detachment

In this plane of existence, the spirit entity will find a quiet place in which to meditate on God. The spirit will seek solitude and will not wish to be in the company of others. In the first vibration of this realm, some may invent a lake that has boats without oars, going in counter-clockwise progression around a small island, symbolic of unwinding and letting go of all thoughts and desires of the physical life left behind. It erases all concepts that are physical. When they reach the shore again, they will step out, shed that spirit body and be lifted up into the Soul Dimension. This will be the final step for that spirit entity's lifetime.

An advanced spirit might go directly to the seventh vibration of this seventh realm, shed the spiritual body and step into the soul. The spirit had already detached from the things of the Earth before exiting its physical body.

Landi: What would some of the other frequency levels within this seventh realm be like?

Raphael: *While the slower frequency levels always relate to the Physical Dimension, the higher levels will concentrate on oneness with God in quiet meditation.*

Landi: As souls develop, must they pass through each of the spirit realms to complete their education?

Raphael: *All spirit realms will be visited at one time or another before the soul's education is completed. In the beginning, their spirit entities will visit one or two realms of interest and skip others altogether, going directly to the seventh realm when their time in the Spirit Dimension is complete. This is because they are not at all inter-*

ested or ready for the information within those other realms. No matter which realm you come from, the seventh realm of the Spirit Dimension is a required step before merging with the Soul Dimension. Some entities who are in their last lifetime of their physical incarnations may skip all realms except the seventh and then go directly to the Soul Dimension. This is because they have no need for any of the others. They will not be manifesting in the Physical Dimension again and will move to an entirely different focus of soul evolution.

Any realm of the Spirit Dimension may be the first stop after death before you make the transition back to your soul. After many, many lifetimes within the physical, the soul has gained great knowledge and wisdom. Each time the spirit exits the physical, it may go directly to the realm of choice. Then, after many more experiences within the physical domain to study the art of creating as God would do, the entity will step beyond the Spirit Dimension and go directly back to the Soul Dimension.

Landi: What assignment is given to a soul after completing all the lessons of physical incarnation?

Raphael: *Some advanced souls are assigned as guides to be of service to other, lesser-experienced souls. These souls are well suited for the task and often use our healing energy. They seek to be of service to mankind. These souls may choose to serve while still within the spirit body of their last incarnation, contacting individuals to suggest ideas and solutions to concerns. Those humans evolved enough to access the Spirit Dimension are well blessed when they have an awareness of their spirit guides. Not all humans choose to make this connection. We encourage each of you to do so.*

Although there is specific training for spirit guides, we remind you that they, too, are evolving spirits who have passed over and are still learning.

Landi: Are there spirit guides who have not completed the physical incarnation cycle?

Raphael: *Yes. Some may be still incarnating as well and may be a favorite teacher in your life or a counselor. You know them only as wise and gentle people.*

Some spirits cross over and assume the role of guide without the training or knowledge to do so. They spout their opinions and viewpoints that are not entirely truth as we would view it. And yet, they give truth as they see it, you understand.

Landi: How do these spirits get away with that? Isn't someone watching their conduct?

Raphael: *Yes, of course. Nothing happens that is not in God's awareness. Communication between the Spirit and Physical Dimensions is a valuable interchange. Once a spirit discovers the "Light," it may wish to "save" a friend still in the physical from the same mistakes it made and would therefore "preach" warnings. This is indeed allowed. It serves both souls in their ever broadening education. Real spirit guides never preach or insist that anyone follow their suggestions. Therefore, always ask for the highest wisdom when contacting those in the Spirit Dimension. Your loved ones who cross over do not always have that wisdom as yet.*

The training for a spirit guide includes many lifetimes of service, both in the Physical Dimension and in the fourth spirit realm. When they incarnate they will choose bodies that will help and console and teach others. When their training is complete, they will first be allowed to work with beginner souls. Later, as they gain wisdom through advanced training, they will be allowed to work with more advanced souls.

Landi: Does everyone have a spirit guide and a Council of Elders?

Raphael: *Most certainly. Most have two or more spirit guides, plus their Council and angels as well. We have said that each human has a whole cheering section in the Spirit Dimension.*

Landi: People talk about the Akashic Records. Where and what are they?

Raphael: *This name, "Akashic Records," refers to the "Life Books" that represent every detail of each physical incarnation. You might say this is your life review. Yet, again, it is just the Mind of God, where all things are recorded. Most people think of it as a separate book for each person. Some have thought of it as a realm or a place where these large, life-story books are kept and, indeed, the guides may show it so. But in reality, it is not, any more than your mind is made up of books to denote your memory banks. While your computer brain stores everything—every sense,* *every thought, every intent, every action, this is also recorded in the mind of God. When a psychic or intuitive receives information from that Mind, it is because the soul's guides deemed it so and because the individual entity was of good intent and would not use it for his or her own gain.*

And so, you see, the mind of God in the form of the Akashic Records are available to those who seek to be of service without selfish gain. Since these records are personal, they are not always open to just anyone out of curiosity.

The Hall of Knowledge is not to be confused with the Akashic Records or Life Books. While both are within the mind of God, they are represented as distinctly different things. The Hall of Knowledge is a place of learning information and is not just classrooms and test tubes but anything you can imagine that you desire to learn. You bring to the Spirit Dimension everything you have learned in the physical. This is why it is so important that each entity learns as much as it possibly can while in the Physical Dimension.

Always listen whenever your soul prompts you to learn something new while in your physical incarnation. When you are in the spirit realms, no matter what level, you will create with only the knowledge you bring to it. For example, if you resonate with the second spirit realm and wish to create a garden of flowers, you can only create those that you can imagine. You do not need to know their technical names. You need only have them in your spirit mind's memory banks, you see.

Landi: Can a spirit go to any of the spirit realms?

Raphael: *Only a more advanced soul can access the faster vibrations of each realm of spirit. It can learn more about plants and flowers and choose to study at the Hall of Knowledge with masters of their choosing. Remember, all is created with only a thought, an idea and an imagination, if you will. And so, if a scientist left the physical world feeling that she had not completed her life task, she might gravitate to a laboratory where she can continue to work on that project until perfection is reached. That soul might then reincarnate to complete the experiment.*

Each soul will move throughout the spirit realms, seeking information and experiences according to it's personality as defined by the ray of color. For example, those souls of the purple ray might desire to learn more about the dimension of spirit. Their thirst for knowledge of God will be quenched. Souls in the slower vibration might cre-

ate a church, a synagogue or a temple-like building where they can continue their study in a certain philosophy or religion with Masters in that field. More advanced souls might meet with the Masters of all religions and study about Mastership. Whatever the spirit wishes to know will be given to him.

A spirit from the blue ray energy might wish to study drama or music or some new way of expressing and would gravitate toward those areas of learning.

Landi: Would spirits studying in a temple, for example, be aware of other religions?

Raphael: *Most often not. This is because in the spirit realm, all souls vibrate to the level of like energy and mind for their greatest comfort and growth. On the other hand, advanced souls might welcome study of all religions so as to see the One within All.*

Landi: We hear about people who can see and speak with spirits. How is that communication possible?

Raphael: *It is possible with the help of guides and*

their Council of Elders who act as the liaison between the two dimensions. This bridge between your world and the Spirit Dimension has to be in accordance with the soul's plan for the life. More and more people have made a contract to be of service in this way at this time in the development of the human species.

Both human and spirit choose to make their life's work a connecting of two dimensions. They bring to the human consciousness the reality that they are eternal spirits who will continue after this life has ended. This is a great service for so many who are fearful of death or do not even believe in a hereafter. Cynics will still debunk it.

Many souls who have crossed over want to contact their loved ones but cannot find a "telephone." It is like calling home from across an ocean to let the family know you traversed the sea of the unknown and arrived safely and happily in the Spirit Dimension.

Landi: How long do spirits stay in this dimension?

Raphael: *That depends upon their needs and desires. One may stay for many of your Earth years, while another might only stay long enough to shed the physical thought forms from his spirit suit and* *then move directly back to his soul group.*

There are many opportunities for learning and play in this dimension. It is a necessary part of the soul's development in studying with the spirit entity, since it is still "ensouled" with it. Yet, life on the Soul Dimension is ongoing as well.

Landi: The soul continues working on both dimensions? How can it do that?

Raphael: *Quite easily. You must remember that your soul is a very large being of light that is already merged with your spirit and physical body for each incarnation. It is not difficult for it to divide its energy. When we speak of "merging," we speak of you opening the doors between these dimensions to obtain an awareness of these realities. We have spoken of only three dimensions: the physical, the spirit and the soul. The Mental and Causal Dimensions are a further advancement in the soul's education. And there are still more dimensions beyond that.*

Landi: I would like to learn more about those dimensions, too. And you didn't mention the Angelic Dimension. Is that some place different from the other ones?

Raphael: *Oh, yes, indeed. But for now, dear one, we have only so much information that can be contained in this book. We will say this: the many dimensions beyond those we speak of here are far more reaching in knowledge than your human mind can comprehend at this moment. We also come to you in this manner so that you can obtain the goal of merging with your spirit and soul. In this, you will reach beyond the veil that hides truth from you in that dimension. You will awaken to a far greater wisdom and knowledge that will bring you many blessings.*

Peace beloved. Remember we, your guides, Council and angels are always with you. Call on us.

Angels Are Among Us.

Are You One?

Chapter Six

Life's Stage

Why People Do What They Do

Hotep: *Souls plan the life in many ways besides preparing their physical costume. They enlist other souls to play parts within the life story, much like a stage play. The individual soul will always be the protagonist or star of the show, while other souls will play the antagonists or supporting roles. Again, as with any good story, the main challenges can be between human versus human, human against nature or human against himself.*

Landi: Do souls always incarnate with their own soul group?

Hotep: *Souls usually incarnate with their own soul group playing the supporting roles for the life. Another circle of souls near the same evolvement will add other characters to the story. Each soul also reaches far beyond their "circle of friends" to create a story on Earth's stage.*

Souls discuss the plot for the story among those who will be involved in the drama. The setting and major events are all planned with the help of guides. There will be a flexible timeline when people and events can come together. Then it's our job to bring about those meetings.

Past life experiences affect the present drama. The guides and Council help the soul to balance previously unresolved conflicts, as well as set up the "rewards" for good actions, thoughts and deeds.

Roles are often reversed. While a mother in one life may become the child in the next, an enemy may become a sibling or grandchild. These latter roles bring opportunities for resolution of conflicts but can explain why people even in families do not always get along.

Some souls enter Earth's stage before others, depending upon their individual story line. For example, the mother role has to enter the physical before the child can. Remember, each soul is the "star" of his or her show. Each story centers around the soul and yet dovetails into others at touch-points within the life.

Role reversal is often a theme, especially in love relationships. For example, if the male left the female for another love and the female suffered greatly because she was left destitute with children, that man's soul will take on the role of a woman who experiences a like event of desertion.

Okay, we'll give an example of "good" karma: Joe saves Sally from drowning. In the next lifetime, Sally might feel "compelled" to pay for Joe's college education. We relate this story to show you that everything is balanced, not just what you term "bad" experiences.

Landi: Is that why I have felt compelled to help some people but not others?

Hotep: *Yes. Actions of compassion and service in one life will be returned, making the life flow with many surprising experiences that delight the human entity.*

A theme such as "abandonment" may color many aspects of the life until the human entity releases that fear and forgives those involved.

Another theme might be "failure." It may

seem that no matter how hard the entity tries to succeed, nothing works. This could be a balance of a previous lifetime of success "at any price," where the soul's entity cheated to gain that success.

Another theme in one life may be lack of self love to the point of martyrdom. The next life will balance that with a great need for survival and the challenges will be in that—a story of a man surviving against all odds in a wilderness, for example.

Landi: Some life stories would never make the best seller list. They live; they work; they pay taxes; they die. Whoopee.

Hotep: *It may seem so but the life has great value in the "books" of God's library. Each life is valuable to the soul's progress. You could say that your life is an "open book" for all on this side to see.*

The Law of Love is the basic principal of all experiences. It's important to note that it's not the people or the events that matter in the life. What counts is how the ensouled human reacts to those events. It's the entity's intent that will spin out each life's story. If your intent is anything less than love, it will create disharmony and unpleasant events in the life.

Landi: Are you saying that nothing is hidden from those in spirit?

Hotep: *Nothing! While you and other souls perform your play on Earth's stage, you always have a "full house" of applauding souls in the audience. The veil that hides us from you is like a two-way mirror. We can see you but you can't always see us.*

Landi: Yikes!" Lots of eyes watching us!

Hotep: *Not at all. It is not our intent, dear ones, to be a "peeping Tom." We don't see things the way you do. We see with the eyes of God's love who sees only beauty and goodness. Consider us as many cheering fans, urging you on to success in your soul's performance. We've always said that you're not alone. We're guiding you even in your sleep.*

Landi: Speaking of sleep, in a dream Rae was shown the flower called "Bleeding Hearts." Would you explain that for her, Hotep?

Hotep: *As guides, we often use dreams to communicate with those we counsel. When Rae awoke from this dream that we sent to her, we urged her to the computer. We explained the symbology of that lovely flower as representing your world of bleeding hearts. It is our desire, with Raphael, the healing Archangel, and your Council of Elders to soothe and comfort all those who mourn over lost loved ones, either from death, desertion or divorce.*

It's always painful to lose one who is deeply loved. The emotional, mental and even physical pain can devastate an individual, pulling him into inertia and despair. Ah, dear ones! You've forgotten your souls. Remember that you are eternal. Death releases your spirit from the shell it has discarded. It rises up and rejoices in its freedom from pain, illness and discomfort.

The process of death and dying is a great teacher of the elements of God. For those who can detach and let go of the material things of your world, they will gain great wisdom and joy in the death transition.

To illustrate our point, we speak of one who suffered from cancer and believed that someone on our side would "save" her with a miracle. She steadfastly refused to believe that she might die. In fact, she feared that if anyone approached her about death, it might jinx the formulae that she had worked out to heal herself. That mystical recipe was to surround herself with "positive-thinking" individuals who would support her belief and therefore give strength to her "miracle." When anyone suggested that perhaps God was calling her home, she angrily sent them away, telling them not to return unless they held the belief that she would be cured. She forgot her soul and her oneness with God that would have allowed her to see everyone as perfect. She was blinded to this truth because she didn't want to leave her young family, fearing that no one could take care of them as well as she could. Fortunately, as the cancer progressed, she resolved herself to her impending death and began to let go of the physical world.

Another person died a most beautiful death. His loving wife had tended to his needs for years as his body declined. The man had seen to it that his affairs were in order and that his wife would have no debts to pay because of him. When it was time for his passing, his wife called their children around him. They said their goodbyes, blessed one another and rejoiced in the knowledge that they would meet again on the other side.

The difference between these two deaths

was not a lack of belief in the other side but rather a fear of losing your side. The woman didn't want to lose her family and the life she had acquired. Although a very spiritual woman, she didn't want to let go. On the other hand, the man had released all attachment to the things of your world and was eager to be free from it.

Death is just a transition from one dimension to another. No big deal. It's a continuation of the soul's journey through the study of the elements of creation.

We say to you: Death is a far easier door to open than is birth when the soul descends into that tiny child and must endure the confinement of a helpless body.

Death is the
"Exit Sign"
That hangs over your lives
From the moment you opened
The "Enter Door"
Called Birth.

Landi: Some people yearn to go "Home." They would gladly give up all of this "stuff" for the peace and joy of being in God's constant presence.

Hotep: *But they already are. Don't you know? Ah, yes, we understand how people in your dimension forget that and yearn for the peace of this side. Yearning for peace is good, for they begin the process of letting go of all desire to manifest in the material dimension. Being fully in your world, each moment, enjoying its joys and its tears is a far greater thing to do than sit around and yearn for the other side. Your play is ongoing. As your saying goes: "Break a leg!" Be the success you desire to be and listen for the applause from our side.*

Now—on the subject of "Desertion," it's a word we use to describe what happens when, for a multitude of reasons, individuals leave your life. This pain of loss is not as great as death but can cause pain nonetheless. Friends come and go in your life. Some seem to just fade with time and distance. Others are wrenched away because of a misunderstanding. Still for others and more so in this time of history on your planet, it is simply because of spiritual growth.

Landi: Growth? That's supposed to be a good

thing. Desertion isn't.

Hotep: *But it is a good thing from your soul's perspective. You happen to see it differently. When one individual steps upon a path of change and the other does not, a separation is inevitable. The one who has not changed might feel deserted by a companion who has. The desertion begins with mental and spiritual changes and spills out into physical changes.*

With spiritual unfolding, greater wisdom leads the soul to seek more challenges and different avenues of learning. That means a change of mind and of interests, which can lead to the separation of relationships. For example, one leaves grade school friends for those of high school and then those friends are left behind for new ones at college. Some create new friendships because of a new job. Parents often feel deserted when their children leave home to be on their own. Anyone who feels that they have been left behind experiences the pain of desertion and abandonment. From our viewpoint, it's your golden opportunity for spiritual growth. You, too, must move on to the next challenge that is set before you.

All Life Is made up of Change

Beginner and even intermediate souls in the physical do not adjust easily to change. They seek comfort in their bodies and in their minds. Anything that disrupts that comfort creates fear and disharmony within them. They'll lash out at the people who have disrupted that comfort zone, driving a wedge even deeper.

Landi: And yet, I've heard some say that divorce is sometimes more painful than death.

Hotep: *Divorce is a painful separation, causing many bleeding hearts on your planet. They're increasing during this time of great changes. In some cases, the separation from a relationship that seemed to be a permanent life event began with the planning of the life before you were born.*

Landi: Are you saying that divorces are sometimes planned before we're born?

Hotep: *Yes, we are. Most often the divorce is the*

result of a previous lifetime that concluded its drama in the present one. Once concluded, it unravels and seems to no longer fill either party's needs. And, indeed, it doesn't. While you hold the belief in relationships lasting "until death do you part," God knows that growth and advancement can be stifled if that dictum is followed without the ability to adjust to change.

Do not misunderstand. In the human condition, two people need to honor their contract of mutual support and respect or their divine plan would not manifest. A binding contract is especially beneficial for the children to have any kind of stability. With the first challenge, the partners would give up.

Landi: I guess divorce can feel very much like desertion, too.

Hotep: *All bleeding hearts feel the same. They bleed and the wounds take a long time to heal.*

Yet, we say to you: the soul undergoes an exacting education that is wide reaching and thorough. Yet, no one fails. No one is retained. There is only advancement. There's nothing within the physical experience that is judged. All experience is golden in the wisdom gained for the soul. It ex-

periments with God's energy, forming scenarios in which to act and react, in which to gain knowledge of all things.

And yes, marriage or the commitment of two people to live and learn together is the greatest challenge of them all.

Landi: Why is the divorce rate so high—over 50% of today's marriages fail.

Hotep: *That's because life is changing four times faster than even fifty years ago.*

The Consequences of Choices Have Speeded Up.

Although linear time hasn't speeded up, the consequence of choices or as you call "Karma" has. What might have taken years to evolve now can take only months. And so, when one person in a marriage or partnership sets foot upon a path of change and the other refuses to join that path as well, there can be a fork in the road that each must travel. This can lead to separation and divorce.

Tiny moment-by-moment choices create divorces and dissolution of partnerships. For example, if Jane and Joe Doe come to a fork in the road, choices must be made. The plot of their play may be written for separation but it does not have to be so. The actors do not know this challenge is coming. Yet Joe's inner senses tell him so. If he acts out of fear of change, he'll cling to Jane with such tenacity that she can't breathe. He'll question her actions, feeling deserted and abandoned before it's even occurred. That anxiety turns to anger, which spills out over Jane like the molten lava of an erupted volcano. Jane singes and stings, building up her wall of protection for the next spill. She feels unjustly accused and retaliates in anger as well. Joe reacts to that with still greater anger, feeling unjustly treated and he builds his own wall. These walls block the ability for either of them to communicate, to reach out to one another in love and heal the wounds. The separation process has begun.

On the other hand, divorce could have been avoided, if, when Joe sensed changes in Jane, he compassionately urged her to make those changes, supporting her in them, even if they were not comfortable for him. In honoring one another as God, they respect each other's need to change. In this way, they would grow together into even greater delights of marital bliss.

Landi: I know of some marriages where the partners go their separate ways but remain married. They "let their partner do their own thing." Is this a healthy relationship?

Hotep: *No. There's very little soul growth between two people who avoid one another. They occupy the same space simply for the comfort of financial security. Growth is stifled out of fear of change.*

Ah! Change is the most feared, yet most obvious presence in each life. We don't offer a balm for the pain caused between two people who once loved one another and now do not. We don't offer a fix that will save a marriage or partnership. We urge you to grow through the pain, grow through the change and become all that your soul seeks for you to be.

There are those who say they've been "burned" through the experience of divorce. We say to you: the disharmony began when one partner depended solely upon another for their com-

fort and joy. Of course, they didn't find it. They became disillusioned. It is not the responsibility of one marital partner to "make" the other happy. It's each person's responsibility to make himself happy. When each person learns to communicate needs without putting blame on the other, they will grow in harmony and peace within self and strengthen the relationship.

Some partners focus on the sexual pleasures of the body and, therefore, when that wanes, they think they've "fallen out of love."

When you're in connection with the higher power of your soul and God, you experience joy. That joy is expressed through playfulness and freedom from inhibitions in the sharing of minds, bodies and souls with one another. In this, humans will know the complete trust of vulnerability and will be filled with the joy of God. We say this to you because the majority of humans on the planet are experiencing the pleasures of the body for their own selfish desires, not to rejoice in the Oneness that is God. Consequently, their experience falls short of their expectations. It becomes a "performance" to pleasure the other person, not a dance of joy. By not giving thanks to God for the gift of that joyous sexual pleasure, they create a monster and their thirst is never satisfied. They are like lost pilgrims searching for the Holy Grail of physical pleasure. In human terms, love means a partner fulfilling needs, instead of a partner rejoicing with them in the uniqueness of their coupling and giving acknowledgement and praise to God for it.

Know this: we do encourage two people who have joined together for comfort and love to work through the differences between them. This exercise is a "fast track" toward spiritual growth, speeding your way home through the encounter of everyday living with another person.

In any relationship between two people, compromises must be made. Each must bend to the other's needs from time to time. Yet, there are traps to this give and take. Because one partner may bend easier than the other, it sometimes becomes expected. Marriage is like a tree, with the partners and children limbs of that tree. When one limb is expected to do all the bending, it finally breaks and the tree is damaged. That doesn't mean that the tree can't be saved. It's the same with a marriage. Each person must seek the greater good to continue the flow of love that creates life-giving energy. If there are no changes or compromises, the love turns to anger that saps the life from the tree of marriage. It will no longer serve the individuals for soul growth and will be cut down. This is the way of life in the physical domain.

Marriage constantly gives the entities an opportunity to choose love and selflessness. It teaches compromise. It teaches self love. It teaches sacrifice. It has an uncountable number of gifts in even the most wretched joining of two people.

When each individual in the partnership can live as though separate, taking care of his or her own needs and yet live together under one roof, they hold that house together with the strength of mutual love and respect. While they remain as individuals following the truth of their own inner guidance, they learn the wisdom that one's guidance cannot interfere with the other's.

As we have said before, non-interference means letting go of the belief that your partner is there to make you happy. Only you can do that for yourselves, dear souls. You are totally responsible for your own decisions and the next experience they create. You'll learn that it can't be for the constant fulfilling of another person's needs. The moment that it is, the marriage is weakened.

We are sad to say that 90% of all marriages on planet earth are based on needs for physical comfort that become expectations put upon the other person. "You take out the garbage." "You take care of the car." "You take care of the house." "You cook the food." "You will make love to me when I need it." Those are the expected roles.

Expectations Can be the Death Of Relationships.

Society imposes roles as well. If, for example, the woman makes more money than the man, the man can become confused in his role as "breadwinner" due to the expectations that society has put upon him. This weakens the fabric of the marriage. On the other hand, if the man thinks of himself more valuable to the marriage than his wife because he's that "breadwinner," tyranny is the result. As always, the Law of Love and God's element of balance are the answer to inner peace. Respect for that inner peace will be the guide in decision making and compromises.

Landi: What about people who compromise the

marriage to death?

Hotep: *Ah yes. There are those, too. They bend and bend until they're broken and no longer useful to the relationship or themselves. Then they feel cheated because they believe they've made all the 'sacrifices' to keep the marriage together. And indeed, it may seem so. In reality, out of fear of loss, they had sabotaged the relationship by not being true to their original self that attracted the partner in the first place.*

But then, too, it can be the reverse. To attract a mate, some might put on a false personality. After the certificate is signed, the real self emerges and the marriage begins to crumble.

Ah! Life is puzzling, is it not? The deceived partner becomes confused and believes that she has done something to create this change, acting out of a false guilt.

Landi: What's "false guilt?"

Hotep: *False guilt is feeling responsible for something over which you had no control, like being late and causing someone aggravation, although your intent was not to do so. Many choices* *within a partnership are made out of a sense of false guilt. It serves no purpose. Real guilt motivates the person to change, to seek forgiveness, to forgive self.*

Do not expend
Any energy over
False Guilt!

On the other hand, the "Blame Game" creates false guilt. Let's say that Harry always wants to exonerate himself by blaming Susan. He projects that blame by being angry toward her. Susan reacts with false guilt, trying to figure out what she did wrong and trying to soothe Harry's anger. He says, "If you hadn't done that..., I wouldn't have done this. It's all your fault." But she isn't at fault. Susan had no intention of creating discomfort for Harry. She was simply his scapegoat. False guilt traps her into believing that maybe if she had done something differently, Harry would be happy.

Yet, we say to you, some relationships are like oil and water; they just don't fit properly. There's nothing wrong with either person. When a marriage "fails," many will jump into the "Blame

Game," to find an excuse for their definition of a "failed marriage."

Landi: Why are some people caught up in a relationship as if they had been sent into it with blinders on?

Hotep: *That's because they were. Their Council of Elders brought them together with "blinders" on. If they had known ahead of time what would happen, they would have turned and run like scared rabbits. The Council helps the soul complete unfinished experiences from past lifetimes.*

It would be wrong for anyone to feel guilty about what they must do for their own soul's growth. Be warned against anyone who uses guilt to control or subdue your spirit for their own personal need for comfort or their fear of change.

We say this to you sternly: it is not good for the physical body to hold on to guilt and resentment. It is wasted energy. It is better to remember that you are all divine and the divine works through you constantly. It is also an opportunity for you to speak your mind that is truth as you see it. To do that, you must know your mind. When you are hurting, you speak and act from the emotional body, not the rational mind.

Do not stress about the failure of a relationship. Angels and guides reach out to each person surrounding any death, desertion or divorce. That includes the children, as well as friends and relatives.

You have the power to become your greatest you. So do it! We say that you can change and move and become anything that God wishes you to be in any moment in time.

Souls get caught up on your planet and build layers of fear and anxiety over needing another to love them. Those layers of fear prevent their guides and angels from getting the message through to them that they are loved. They need not look to another human for the perfect love that comes only from God and dwells right inside them.

As soon as each of you can peel off the layers of fear that a relationship or anyone may hurt you, then you begin to heal. No one can hurt you unless your soul has chosen to experience that hurt as a balance from hurting another.

By merging with your soul, you'll see that bigger picture. You'll be better able to let go of your hurts and begin to trust that your soul has a plan for your life that supercedes your own narrow vision.

****

Hotep: *We will speak today on the dynamics of group interaction on Earth's stage. In every assembly, each individual plays a certain role that reflects his soul's personality. We'll give these roles specific titles to help you understand each position in the group. Each role has a positive or negative influence upon the group according to the soul's level of advancement.*

The Leader or Facilitator – *This soul is usually from the red, orange or blue ray. He'll make decisions for the group to keep it focused and moving. For example, the leader might say, "We'll meet once a week. Our agenda will be..."*

- ***Positive****: He'll bring all viewpoints forward and yet stay neutral.*
- ***Negative****: He'll act like a tyrant who insists that things be done his way.*

The Antagonist – *This person can always find the loophole, the part that may go wrong and will warn the group to beware. He's valuable in bringing balance to the positive-negative poles. The antagonist can be from any of the seven rays. He'll say, "Well, yes but..."*

- ***Positive****: He brings the opposite view-*

point, pointing out pitfalls and possible problems.

- ***Negative**: He's a pessimist or cynic who debunks ideas before they're born.*

***The Protagonist** – This soul is often the one who came up with the idea in the first place. He will optimistically believe that the group can accomplish their goals and will encourage forward movement in spite of obstacles. He might say, "We can do it. Let's just put our heads together and find a solution to this problem."*

- ***Positive**: He brings enthusiasm for the basic idea; encourages and seeks the positive viewpoint but he's realistic.*
- ***Negative**: He's unrealistic and can be an over-zealous rebel.*

***The Recorder** – This person will bring order amidst confusion. He's most likely from the red, orange, yellow or blue rays. He might say, "That's a good idea. I'll write it down."*

- ***Positive**: He keeps track of actual events and words.*
- ***Negative**: He shows opinionated and slanted reporting.*

The Server *– This green ray soul is concerned for the group's physical welfare, asking, "Does anyone need coffee while I'm up?"*

- ***Positive****: He's willing to take care of people's physical and emotional needs.*
- ***Negative****: He becomes a slave to others just to achieve approval. He does not value his own views.*

The Activator *– This soul of the red, orange or blue ray will find the next step and be ready to take action. He'll say, "We can call... and they'll do it. Or we can..."*

- ***Positive****: He'll find a way to make things happen for the benefit of all.*
- ***Negative****: He acts as a bully who pushes everyone to make things happen his way regardless of the consequences.*

The Star Searcher *– This soul of the indigo ray will find a unique and different way to accomplish the group's goal, saying, "Wouldn't it be great if..." or if he's of the purple ray, he might suggest that the group say a prayer before beginning each session to call upon the "Higher Powers" for guidance.*

- ***Positive****: He can think out of the box;*

can pull in unusual ideas in problem solving.

- ***Negative**: He's a dreamer who is unrealistic.*

Although we use the pronoun, "he," each of these roles can also be enacted by a "she." As in every relationship between two or more people, male/female roles divide and sometimes switch back and forth. Male roles would tend to be the Leader/Facilitator, the Antagonist and the Activator. Female roles would tend toward the Protagonist, the Recorder, the Server and the Star Searcher.

Don't misunderstand: we don't mean that the male energy is better or lesser than the female. We refer to the male qualities of strength, assertiveness, decisiveness, action orientation and bravery. In the female energy we see the gifts of passivity, compassion, nurturing, understanding and creativity. These energies can be exhibited in both male and female entities at alternating times.

Each entity brings to the group unique energy that will blend and enhance and energize everyone or it will detract, distract, drain and scatter energy. Yet, every group combination serves God in that it challenges individuals to grow in pa-

tience, compassion, knowledge and unconditional love. These "virtues" are necessary for the advancement of each soul in the School of Creation.

We are done. Peace.

What On Earth Are You Creating?

Chapter Seven

The Truth . . . . .

About Health

Hotep: *In your physical world, life is a game of Truth or Consequences. When you follow the truth of the Law of Love, the consequences are happiness, harmony and health. When you break that law, there are the unpleasant consequences of depression, disharmony and illness.*

Landi: Okay, Hotep, who broke the Law of Love when they polluted our world with exhaust fumes, toxic waste and food so filled with other chemicals? Is there any hope for good health in that kind of a world?

Hotep: *The Law of Love was broken because of the "bottom line" money and greed.*

But of course there's always hope. Many of your kind are already solving the problems of that toxic waste and the chemicals in your food. Have you not obtained the right to read the ingredients on labels? This is a forward movement toward good health. And more factories are cleaning up their toxic wastes and the air pollution they've caused. You and others have demanded and have received these changes.

No, good health is not an impossible goal. Each must do their own part to reach that goal. One way to take care of the physical body is to eliminate the bad habits of poor nutrition and a sedentary life style that creates a cushion or the "spare tire," around your emotional body. Soothing your emotional body may come in the form of eating comfort foods, such as sweets. It also comes in relying on acts of comfort, such as sleep or other escape mechanisms. Some of these comfort actions are in direct opposition to a healthy lifestyle.

Remember: you are the creator of your world. When there is harmony between your soul and you, health in mind, body and spirit is the natural result. Once you have merged with your soul and God, you will indeed find that your health will improve daily.

To merge with your soul, it is imperative to live in the moment that we shall call, "Now Time." When you focus on the task at hand, with your intent to do the very best that you can in that moment, you will be given information that will keep your physical and spiritual bodies in sync with each other and in good health.

Let us give an example. On the way to work, the traffic is backed up and the exhaust fumes billow all around you. You can't do anything about it in that moment. You could choose to rant and rave, joining others in your "road rage," and building stress that will cause illness. Or, you could choose to close your windows, turn on your radio or CD player and listen to soft, gentle music that soothes your nerves. The latter reduces stress, creating balance within your mind, spirit and body. In so doing, you learn the art of creating health.

Landi: But it's so easy to fall into bad habits that are hard to break, like eating fast foods while on the run, or grabbing that candy bar for energy.

Hotep: *We say to you, dear ones, health is a daily*

habit that has to be established moment-by-moment, first in the mindset and then in the body's actions. The habits of eating whole foods and of exercising daily, will create health. Since most people on the planet seek only comforts and pleasures in the body, they abandon any type of exercise and any food that does not please them. Some achieve pleasure from the melatonin of extreme exercise such as running. Yet, running can cause the body side effects of damage to the cartilage in the knees, ankles and hips. There is a consequence to every action, as you well know.

Many of your world experience loneliness and loss, turning to food and self-indulgences for comfort. These escape hatches cause damage to their bodies and in turn increase their sense of frustration—like that "vicious circle" that traps a soul in one place without moving forward. Each lifetime is given challenges to move your soul forward. When you open to your inner voice to do what is healthy for you in any given moment, you can break that vicious circle.

Let us make suggestions in how to avoid that vicious circle, thereby creating harmony for all who would read this.

Eight Keys to Health

True Prayer

Establish a routine of praising God many times a day. Some say, "An attitude of gratitude" is the way to do it. We agree. When the mind focuses on finding the good in all things, in praising God for the gifts of life, then the person's vibrations are raised and the body can heal itself.

True prayer always begins with praise of the One that created All That Is. A joyous heart begins the merging with the soul and its guides and angels to bring the individual into harmony with the universe.

A Mind
Filled with praise of
God
Creates health.

There are those upon the planet who have a multitude of methods of speaking to God and a multitude of names for the One. Each religion has a prescribed method of prayer. We say to you: each is valid. Each is necessary for the development of the soul in that moment in time.

Souls set up the human entity to be programmed into a religious belief, a political belief, a familial belief, a social belief and a patriarchal belief. All of these set up the attributes and/or challenges for the life. When the human merges more fully into the awareness of his soul and God, he may begin to question present beliefs. The person might question God, "You said such and such was truth. Now I find that it is not so."

And, of course, God says nothing.

Your soul is always trying to expand your truth about God and the universe, until you can see everyone and everything as God. In another lifetime, you may have experienced one rigid set of beliefs. In this lifetime, you are searching. You might find in studying all religions that although they are not the same, they have the same intent of rising above physicality and merging with the spiritual self and God.

Do not plead for your needs when you pray. It implies that God will not or cannot fill them. This type of prayer is made through the vibration of fear. Instead, lift up your heart and rejoice that your needs are already a reality. Remember: your "needs" are not for physical "things." They are for sustenance, peace, har-

mony, laughter, good friends, good work that rewards you with just pay and of course, love.

Rejoice in being who you are, a magnificent creature, perfectly expressing God in this moment in time. This is a hard concept, for each religion sees God a different way. It is difficult for these concepts to be melded into One Source, One Creator, One Concept of all being united into One.

It is the nature of the human—to question, to label, to categorize. How else would you learn? It is good to question. It is good to be the skeptic. It is not good to be a cynic. A cynical person has already made up his mind.

Our common denominator in all this variety is that each human in any race, color or creed has a soul created by God. Souls are a fraction of God's essence and therefore to be honored as one with God.

True Work

Work stimulates the mind and body to create beauty and order in the world. Many people hate their jobs and it becomes true slavery rather than true work. The former can create illness and depression. The latter brings the individual a sense of accomplishment and joy. It has been said that if you can do what you love to do and get paid for it, you are truly blessed. This is True Work. For some it might be their "hobby" that becomes a joyous source of income only after retirement.

Unfortunately, with the economy of your present-day world, many people have to work just for the paycheck and some do not even have any source of income. In some countries, work for pay is almost nonexistent. Survival is all consuming. Yet, each person has created the circumstances that will gain the most wisdom for his soul. Remember, dear ones, you can't judge another by looking from the outside in. This poverty brought into the world a Mother Teresa and many more like her. The poor were as much of a gift to her, as she was to them. Those working for the Peace Corps or the Red Cross have agreed to serve those in need. The cycle of life continues with each person being served for their greatest good.

It is important that you don't judge another's circumstances. Instead, if you see a wrong and are motivated to make it right, do it. That is its purpose in your life.

That "attitude of gratitude" goes a long way. No matter what your situation, being the owner of a company or sweeping floors for bread, we suggest that you create a joyful attitude toward work, focusing on each moment to perform your duties with perfection. Give thanks for the opportunity to bring laughter and joy to those around you. Give full attention to the work, doing the very best you can. The integrity of this attitude will lift you out of the ordinary and bring you into True Work.

Conversely, a person can focus so intensely upon his job that he becomes a chronic workaholic, neglecting his family and his own health to follow the rigid path he has set up for self. He becomes caught up in his work, identifying with his job that gives him an outlet for creativity or allows him to provide the pleasures of life. This creates an imbalance that creates illness—and sometimes divorce.

True Rest

Creating time for rest, not just sleeping at night but resting during the day, is a necessary element for balance. When neglected, it increases stress, thus causing illness within the body and mind. Rest means going away from the work, seeking silence and inner calm. Even in the workplace, you can find a place to rest. If each person went into the "Restroom" and followed that name's advice, by sitting quietly for a few minutes, relaxing the mind and body, it would live up to its name.

Rest and sleep restore the life energy and rejuvenate the body, allowing it to recharge its batteries within the Soul's larger energy. Although it's not the best way, many people may rest by watching an uplifting movie. Rest doesn't occur when watching an action-oriented one that has violence. This discharges the vital energy of the body and mind.

For some, true rest can be obtained through a short "power nap" where the mind and body are totally relaxed. This isn't possible for most people due to daily schedules. Therefore, we recommend periodically taking slow deep breaths to reenergize. Also, spend at least ten minutes in serious relaxation, going inward to relax every muscle and every fiber of your being. Then allow another ten minutes in that deep state of relaxation to be with us—your guides and helpers. Nothing need be said. Just be.

Through these modalities, you can also obtain the kind of rest that is equivalent to a full night's sleep. Many yogi's do not sleep because they can meditate so deeply that they leave their bodies and go home within their soul for rejuvenation.

A restful night's sleep is the best. If some

physical ailment breaks up that sleep, you can feel disoriented and exhausted. You need to go through the ninety-minute sleep cycle that slows the mind's brain waves. During this cycle, your spirit goes through the Alpha vibration, where your soul can help you through dreams. Next, your spirit goes through the Theta vibration, where you can travel in your spirit body anywhere on the planet or beyond. Then you go into the Delta vibration, where you can go to the Soul Dimension for awhile. This is one-half of the sleep cycle. It then reverses itself, bringing you back to wakefulness at the end of the ninety-minute period. But most will not wake and will simply slip back into the next cycle. Without this deep sleep, you can become ill and restless and unable to think clearly.

Landi: What about those people with chronic sleep disorders?

Hotep: *Some may need to find a doctor who will prescribe helpful medical or holistic modalities; others may find meditation or hypnosis helpful. Still others find "white noise" helps. It may be your soul's plan to keep you searching for help, thus bringing you to the people you are to meet* *and interact with during your lifetime. You may be instrumental in bringing about a new discovery that helps others with the same problem.*

True Play

A playful attitude grounds you within your soul's energy. This is found in whatever brings you laughter and fun. It could be playing board games or cards with friends or creating something beautiful or taking a walk in nature or dancing or singing or playing sports. However, play can become work by adding competition or too much mental and physical effort. True play requires physical exercise and physical movement; therefore, sitting in front of the television or watching a movie doesn't count. It also doesn't include a physical "workout" in a gym. That's work!

Open your
Mind and heart
Each day
To the joy of
Nature around you.

A walk in nature can bring true play. Na-

tive Americans looked at a bird and saw the Great Spirit in that tiny creature. Let it speak to you of spirit, of peace, of joy. Place yourself within the breath of nature to replenish your lungs and your body with the nutrients of life that nature can give to you.

Creating a time for play can unfortunately become stressful for many. The planning of a vacation to experience a whirlwind of activities, with the rushing to get from place to place in a limited amount of time or the rush to play hard, so as not to miss a single opportunity to experience everything offered, all adds up to more stress and a defeat of the whole purpose of play.

On the other hand, there are those action-oriented souls who delight in this kind of frantic adventure. Depending upon their soul age, they relish the kinds of activities that offer challenges and competition. For them it is true play.

While action-oriented play may be more suitable for red, orange and yellow ray souls, it can become a source of stress for souls in the higher vibrating rays of green, blue, indigo and violet.

True Knowledge

In focusing your soul's energy through your mind, your desires and ideas can become amazing creations and accomplishments. All new ideas come from God through us, your guides and angels. We always encourage you to increase your knowledge.

Whenever an idea surfaces,
For you to gain new knowledge,
Follow it through.
It is your soul
Knocking on your door.

True knowledge could happen through an idea that sends you scurrying to the Internet to research more information. It could be a creative idea that touches your heart and makes you want to tuck it inside like a precious jewel to take out in the future. It could occur through a book that challenges you to think again, moving you out of previous belief ruts. True knowledge, by true study, opens your mind to new ideas, helping you to hear your soul's voice from within, while also helping you to really believe in yourself. It opens your mind to the presence of angels around you and to God.

True Love

Everyone is looking for "True LOVE." It begins by loving self without judgment, blame, or condemnation. A loving attitude helps you to accept your life, your physical body, your talents—everyone has them—and every experience as a gift of God's Unconditional Love. It requires a large dose of trust in acknowledging and blessing all that you are. Through gratefulness, you gain access to your soul, who with the help of angels and your Council of Elders, created every tiny part of you. This Higher Mind experiences your every thought, word and deed. It gains knowledge and wisdom from even the smallest of your dramas, both what you call "good" and "bad." Trust this.

True Love
Acknowledges
God
Within Self.

Everyone seeks their "true love" in another person who will become a life partner. We say: seek true love first in self and the joyous aura you create will draw that true partner to you. The contrary happens when one continually stresses over finding someone, fearing that no one will love them or find them attractive. It only attracts another with like fears.

It is not healthy for individuals to try to blend one another's personalities in a relationship just for the sake of being loved. It is healthy for individuals to come together in mutual agreement to be faithful to their soul's definition of self. Only then can two people live in harmony with one another.

True Nourishment

Treat your body to whole foods. By this we mean foods that have been grown without chemicals—organically as some would call it. Whenever possible, grow your own vegetables. Can or freeze them for a year's supply. We know for some this is impossible—especially if you live in a city. But more and more farmers are growing foods organically. Buy these foods to support this healthy effort.

The way to break compulsive eating is through daily meditation. The subconscious mind needs to be reprogrammed. In a deep meditative state, the individual gives praise to God and then praise to self that is spirit and soul. Observe the good that the soul has created within the body that serves it faithfully. "Love thyself" needs to be the daily motto. This is not "self-centeredness," but is rather honoring God who dwells within and has created the you to bring peace and harmony into the world.

Good Food Creates Good Health.

Landi: What about those people that cannot seem to lose weight even if they eat healthy?

Hotep: *Sometimes weight loss is not possible because excess weight in itself is perhaps a balancing of a previous lifetime of starvation. The entity can do nothing to change the condition until the soul is satisfied that the past life has been balanced.*

Landi: How can we communicate with our souls that we need to remedy the situation for our present body's health?

Hotep: *By doing just that...speaking to your soul in this manner and suggesting—never demanding—that perhaps you both have learned the lesson and can now release it.*

Landi: Which healing modality would be best: "traditional" with doctors of medicine or "alternative" with chiropractic, holistic or naturopaths?

Hotep: *Whichever method occurs to you in the specific moment for the specific dis-ease is correct. We emphasize the necessity to listen to your soul or as some would say, your sixth sense. Would that all peoples on your planet have faith in their inner senses, their bodies would rejuvenate naturally and continue to serve them without pain or illness.*

Let us reiterate regarding the healing and increased health of the body. The key to health is joy. To create joy, you must merge first with your spirit, your soul and then God. When there is complete trust and faith that God is pure love, ready to shower peace and joy upon you, then you will know instant health.

In Everything, Balance Is the Key.

Remember that balance is the key word for you and your soul. When illness occurs, some ingredients for balance are missing in the daily routine. The first thing most people neglect is their spirit. Taking time to meditate and pray is put off, yet this is the most essential part of one's day to replenish the body's cells.

For optimal health, you need balance in all things. Therefore, let's summarize: 1) give praise to God each day; 2) meditate daily; 3) walk in nature each day or at least pause for a quiet moment to look out a window and study nature; 4) drink lots of fresh water; feed the body whole foods: whole grains; organically grown vegetables and fruits; meats and poultry that are naturally grain fed, not chemically induced to grow more quickly; and 5) create balance in the life with time for prayer, work, rest and play.

Health is wonderful. The body doesn't need to age when you have merged with God.

Balance Creates Health. Imbalance Creates Illness.

Pastel by Betty Rae

Both Bring Wisdom to the Soul.

Chapter Eight

..... Or Consequences

About Illness

Hotep*:* *Well! How are we feeling today?*

Landi: We're feeling fine. Why do you ask?

Hotep*:* *Because we come today to speak of illness.*

Landi: Oh! Tell me, Hotep, why would God send anyone a debilitating illness?

Hotep: *God does not send the illness, nor does It punish or judge anyone.*

Landi: Then who does? Who up there is in charge of the Illness Department?

Hotep: *You! You are in charge! You are responsible for each and every moment that you create in the physical domain. When the divine Law of Love is ignored, the consequences may result in illness that can damage your human vehicle. While God is the energy through which you create, It has given you and all created entities in the Physical and Spirit Dimensions, free will to create anything you choose—including illness.*

In each life drama, illness creates an excellent opportunity for soul advancement in the study of the laws of creating. You have already discovered that souls come in various sizes, shapes and colors, as do their experiences. Each soul and its human counterpart will see the world through the eye of these events. And so it is the same with illness.

Landi: Whoa! Wait a minute! I would never choose to create an illness.

Hotep: *In your human consciousness you wouldn't but when you ignore the Law of Love, that's what you create. You forget, too, that your soul* *has carefully planned your life and directs you though your mind and body as to what will facilitate that divine mission. Sometimes an illness can help you do that.*

Landi: I'm really trying to understand this, Hotep. What does illness have to do with God's method of creating?

Your moment-by-moment Choices Define your future.

Hotep: *Each person has created illness because of misunderstanding the elements of creation. Remember, the Essence of God is pure unconditional love. Love is the system that continually renews the universe. All the creative elements come from love.*

For example, an element of God's Essence is perfect balance. It creates harmony between the polarities and brings balance into your life and your world. When you are extremely negative or pessimistic, you are out of balance and illness can be the result.

In seeking to share unconditional love with

everyone, God expresses the element of abundance. When you deny love to yourself or another, you stop the flow of abundance. You will experience lack of love and money and then worry about not having enough to go around. This can cause stress that creates illness.

The magnetic energy surrounding you attracts whatever you think and believe. Attraction is another element of God. It returns love when love is projected outward. Withholding love out of fear of rejection or being hurt will attract others with that same fear. An unstable relationship can be the result, which may cause illness. This divine element of attraction is a law of creation.

God's unconditional love sees everything as perfectly expressing Itself—especially you. These elements of God observe creation without judgment or interference. When you judge another, you will bring those who will criticize and judge you. When you interfere in another's choices, you will attract manipulative and controlling people into your life. This, too, can cause illness of the mental or physical body.

When you are expressing the Creator, you are in the element of "Now Time," that recognizes past, present and future as all one within God. By focusing in the moment, you cannot dwell on past errors, nor can you worry about the future. If you insist on dwelling on perceived wrongs done to you without forgiving self and others, you may create illness. Likewise, if you constantly worry about perceived disasters in the future, that can also create illness.

Note: this does not mean that you should never think about the past, nor plan for the future. It means that obsessing about past errors, believing that you cannot change, could create illness. You are a co-creator with God. Learn from the past and create anew. Do plan for the future, making appointments, frugally setting aside money for retirement and so on. But do not obsess when those plans change.

God is a perfect Creator. It sees you as perfect just as you are. Whenever you find imperfection in another, you will find blame and judgment toward self. This can create illness.

When you cannot detach from anything that creates less than divine love, you may build up anger and judgment, creating worry and blame. This can also create illness.

So in answer to your question, "How do these Elements of Creation relate to illness?" we say to you that when you create health, peace, abundance, love, balance and harmony, you are using those elements of God's creative energy correctly. Anything less says that you are not.

Disharmony brings
Illness.
Balance brings
Health.

Landi: Is every illness the result of ignoring these laws of creation?

Hotep: *No. Through an expression of divine love, some souls have agreed to take on a illness to be of service to mankind.*

For example: One entity had Polio as a child. The illness brought her into the hospital to associate with the doctors and nurses. Because of the experience, the woman became a doctor and spent her life in great service to children—at first in the Polio ward with the "Iron Lung," and later with children suffering from arthritis. This is an example of fulfilling a soul's plan for the life.

Landi: How can we avoid breaking the laws of creation when there are no "cops" with flashing blue lights following us? Do we just wait until we get a ticket—illness—and then try to figure out what law we broke?

Hotep: *Good analogy! Figure out how the illness serves you—and it always does. Is it an opportunity to serve mankind, as with the polio victim? Does it give you needed rest? Does it influence a decision that you have avoided making? Any time you are not happy, look within to see where you have ignored God's love and the urgings of your soul. Ask for a reconnection to that reflection of God and you will be amazed at the many ways it will respond—through vivid dreams or books that may drop into your hands or a song that gets stuck in your mind. It could come from a comment from a stranger. Once you are willing to listen and change your path, you will discover new ways to improve your health and erase illness from your life.*

Most importantly, when you realize that God is pure love, that you are made from that love, then you will experience joy, the only true emotion. All the opposite emotions of anger, envy, prejudice, anxiety and hate reflect the entanglement of the physical. They are not reality. They are your "tickets," or consequences, from "breaking" the creative laws. Joy comes from being in the pres-

ence of God. Once you raise your thoughts above the mundane and contact your soul, you will experience that pure love and know joy.

Your soul,
Through you,
Creates with every breath,
Every thought
And every action.

The consequences of every action are the reality of the next breath, the next thought, the next action. Therefore, every thought of kindness, beauty and compassion will come back to you at some future time in the physical as kindness, beauty and compassion.

Whatever you focus upon will multiply, until that is all you can see. Do not focus on those things you label "bad," thinking that is all there is to so-called "Karma." It is not. You will miss all the "Positive Karma" that you have reaped in this life and many others. Focus on what you call good and more of it arrives.

The soul uses many things to bring balance into the entity's experiences. If the human has cre-

ated chaos, the soul seeks harmony. If the person has created lust, the soul seeks celibacy. If the entity has created cruelty, the soul seeks kindness and so on. Likewise, if the entity has created an austere life of solitude, in the future the soul will choose a life surrounded by people. Always there is balance.

An example of the consequences of imbalance would be when a person has experienced overindulgence in food or alcohol. His body will most likely rebel with a sour stomach, headache and fatigue. The body is calling out for balance.

Sometimes the soul's guides and Council will even create an accident or illness simply to slow the entity down, giving it an opportunity to turn within and listen to the soul.

Each person has experienced illness on the physical level and so we say: know that the soul is experiencing the wisdom of it. Illness is a great teacher.

While we don't minimize the suffering caused by illness and disease, we do wish to raise your thoughts and feelings beyond the physical. By merging with your soul and viewing life from that higher perspective of love, joy, peace and harmony, you will understand, accept and erase illness. This will create true health in mind, body and spirit. It will help you let go of your judgments and questions of "why," and allow you to experience all of life with greater knowledge and wisdom.

Landi: It doesn't look as though most people on this planet are doing that.

Hotep: *Not yet. However, more and more are beginning to awaken to their power as co-creators with God. That is the purpose of this book, is it not?*

Landi: Yes, it is. What else can we do to bring others to this "awakening?"

Hotep: *No one is expected to "convert" anyone. Each person has a sacred right to choose either from the positive or from the negative polarity. In so doing, they will experience positive or negative consequences. What a great teacher first-hand experience is!*

Some consequences are a wake-up call. The entity goes along his merry way, making choices and creating his life, until he has an accident or illness that reins in his creating spree. He will not recognize this as a gift of love from

God to bring him back into balance. No, he will blame it on the other guy who smashed his new car or on some germ that attacked his poor, innocent body.

The soul will try very hard to bring the human personality back on the path of balance and love, without resorting to drastic life-changing events. However, when the person persists in following a different course from the one chosen by the soul, sometimes drastic measures must be taken—even death.

Landi: Even death? Why?

Hotep: *Rather than create more need for balancing acts in future lifetimes, the soul may choose to end the life—while its ahead, if you will. Now do not assume that every illness or accident is because of errors in creating. Sometimes an illness or accident is your exit back home that has been planned since the beginning of your time on the planet.*

Landi: How do we know when an illness or an accident is a misdemeanor from ignoring the laws of creation or a felony that is our ticket out of the here?

Hotep: *Most "misdemeanors" are received as warnings through your body that is like a barometer, telling you when it is out of balance. When you pay attention and correct your ways, then your ticket was only a minor infraction. But if you find yourself over here with us, you can be assured that it was a felony!*

Landi: Will we ever learn to play this game of Truth or Consequences without the experience of illness?

Hotep: *In each individual's life, experience has been found to be the best teacher. That's why God has set up this whole system of incarnating on physical planets. Experience equals learning!*

Let us give you another example. A person's career can cause stress to the point of illness. The soul is warning the human to change jobs but when the entity does not, the consequences of that choice can result in a severe illness or perhaps death from a stroke or a heart attack. Everyone hears that inner voice to slow down and change the course of action. Few people listen. The result is illness—or death.

Your soul seeks
To keep you
in the
Peak of health.

In our playfulness, we do not diminish in any way the trials and tribulations of the human experience. We know how difficult it is for humans to understand the benefits of those trials. Yet, we call you to merge with your soul, to see the bigger picture, to rise above it all and see God's plan within it. Study and learn to create using those perfect laws of love.

Always remember that your soul, your angels and those on your Council of Elders, are your helpers throughout the life. Call on us when you are ill. Ask the Archangels for divine wisdom to see and know the right course of action back into health. You will be given the answer. It means reconnecting to that still, small voice within—your soul.

Landi: When we're experiencing a dysfunctional relationship, what laws have we broken?

Hotep: *The "Laws of Creation," as you choose to*

call them are not really laws. As we stated previously, there is only the Law of Love. We speak of the elements of God that express as balance, abundance, perfection and unconditional love. When any of these elements are ignored in a relationship, it becomes dysfunctional or out of balance.

As always we give the example. Those who are in the care-giving role can create discomfort in their own bodies to the point of exhaustion and illness in order to keep their partner from anger or criticism of them or from any kind of disharmony in the home.

When this can no longer be tolerated by the entity, anger begins to erupt within the body through a twisting in the abdomen or tension in the neck and shoulders. Listen to those signals and speak of that discomfort by verbalizing with words like, "I'm not comfortable with that decision. Let's discuss this further." Avoid verbal expressions that can be abusive. Always seek to resolve conflict through love and respect. When that does not seem possible, do not result to illness that gives permission for the servitude to stop. Express your needs in a loving but forceful way, demanding inner harmony and peace for yourself.

The wonderful challenge in a relationship is to follow your own inner guidance of your soul's expression. It is not selfishness when you honor God within you, seeking the greater good for all concerned. But when a partner is abusive, either verbally or physically, you have every right to terminate that partnership immediately, rather than choosing a serious illness or an exit door out of the physical.

Landi: What are some of the exits that souls might choose?

Hotep: *There are hundreds of exits a soul might choose. Look up the death notices in your newspapers. They will speak of a variety of illnesses, all kinds of accidents or simply old age. Yet, we say to you, those were not the cause of the exit.*

A soul may call the entity home when it does not face an unresolved conflict, not just in relationships but in anything like a job or terrible poverty. The conflict was a golden opportunity for growth and change but when the person does nothing other than focus on the problem, the opportunity is wasted. The soul can choose a heart attack, cancer, accident, you name it. There are a whole laundry list of exits.

Yet, we say to you: before a soul enters into the physical, most often it has already planned its exit. Sometimes it will have three to five probable or possible exits in the different periods of the life, depending on whether the agreements come together and are able to be fulfilled. If they are and the soul has accomplished all that it needs, it can choose that exit.

For example, a beginner soul might exit because of fear about the trip into physicality, thus aborting the mission to incarnate. A crib death may be caused by a new soul who had a peek at life in the physical through a tiny helpless form with its stomach growling and its pants wet. The soul might panic and run away, like a little child on the first day of Kindergarten who wants to go home. The soul runs back to where it can move freely and have no discomfort. The decision to abort the mission, however, already has its consequences, as in creating a crisis for the parents who dearly wanted a child. The pain that the soul's decision caused starts the Game of Truth or Consequences and its scorecard must be settled. Therefore, in a later lifetime, the young soul might lose a child and experience tremendous loss. This is not punishment or judgment. It is the rounding out of the soul's education in the emotional experiences of the human condition. One act begets another that balances the first—and so on.

Then, too, a soul may experience an exit through an automobile accident where the spirit is thrown out of the body. The spirit returns to the "Light," but is told that it has to go back; therefore, the spirit is sent back into the body, creating a "near-death" experience. Some may retain a conscious awareness of their out-of-body travel to the "other side," thus widening the perspective of the human's understanding of life and death. This also leaves a door open for the soul to communicate with the human. This is what would be called a "life-changing experience," shifting the entity's viewpoint of everyone and everything. There is an appreciation of others because the human now understands that each person has a spirit and a soul. It is as though they have climbed up several steps and are looking at life from a higher platform.

Souls may choose
A close encounter
of the
"Near-Death" kind.

Landi: Is that considered an "exit," when it didn't result in death?

Hotep: *It sure is. Call it an exit in a revolving door, because the person actually died and was then "resurrected."*

Landi: Regarding exit illnesses, is it permissible to shorten the life of someone suffering from the last stages of a terminal illness such as cancer?

Hotep: *Although it is never good work to shorten the life of a perfectly good body through suicide, it is different for those who would shorten their lives in a long-extending illness. They may choose not to eat in order to end the life sooner or they may choose to take the drug that will ease their pain but shorten the life. This is not suicide. This is humanitarianism.*

And yet, we say to you: the extension of the life of pain serves the soul to either erase the pain of past deeds or to erase the pain that thoughtless humans inflict upon one another. Yes, an entity can offer his pain for others, just as the Master Jesus did. When pain is offered as a balm for a pain-inflicted world, that gift of sacrificial love can create change in the hardened hearts of mankind. It does make a difference. Do not ever forget that.

Like the woman with polio, an illness can

be created to bring together other souls to fulfill a contract made before incarnating. And severe disabilities created from occurrences called "accidents" offer the entity an opportunity for great spiritual growth if they choose to accept it.

A more advanced soul might choose a long-suffering exit, such as cancer, as a way of allowing his family to let go so that he can exit the physical to complete his work in other dimensions. He knew that his family would grieve if, for example, he left quickly because of a heart attack. The sudden severance from the family would not allow them to make an adjustment. In their grief, the family would likely pull on that entity from the other side, begging him to stay near them. But if they see their loved one suffering from an illness over a long period of time, they will be glad for the blessed relief of death. They will have had time to say their good-byes and to let him go.

Landi: What about children who die young? Why would the soul choose that exit when it had hardly begun the life?

Hotep: *As we have said in the beginning, there are as many reasons for death and disease as there are souls. It is always difficult for humans* *with any compassion at all to accept the death or suffering of a child. That in itself could serve as a motivation for an adult to help in some way, which might promote their own growth.*

Innocent children bring to the adults who surround them the gift of love and acceptance. They are an example of God's pure love. On the other hand, you need to remember that just because one is young, it does not mean that his soul is necessarily young. The soul may choose an early exit to balance other lifetimes. Perhaps they choose to give back "good" karma to others through the example of love, such as children with Downs Syndrome. These souls may come in to fulfill a contract or an agreement to help the adults around them comprehend the love of God. The child is innocent, sweet and loving. That is all he knows. He is a gift, not a curse, to the parents and to all who come to know him. Many souls have come in during this time with similar ailments to teach the attribute of love.

As always, there are a multitude of blessings to be gained from any illness, even the so-called sexually transmitted diseases. The lessons learned are invaluable for the human and its soul; mainly, that each person is responsible for each decision that he makes.

No experience
Is wasted.
It brings only wisdom
To the soul.

Again, it is very hard for humans to understand that any illness would be part of the divine plan for souls. They do not see how the soul struggles to get through to their human personality's mind to tell them that there is something beyond the physical pleasures of this world. When the entity finally awakens to his soul and realizes that he is primarily spirit, a great leap of spiritual advancement takes place.

At the end of each physical life, the spirit must account for every single thought, word and deed. This revelation can quickly change the entity, causing him to think twice before he creates upon the planet in the future.

There is never just one reason for illness or death. The soul does not choose illness for itself alone. Each person's life reverberates outward and touches many others. Often, being of service to others, either as the caregiver or patient, will bring an opportunity for soul advancement.

When you spend time daily going inward to merge with your soul and God, there is less need for illness. The divine guidance will direct you to do what is necessary for health. Again, unfortunately, most people do not do this and never learn to hear that "inner voice." That inner wisdom will caution you not to expend your energy without replenishing it daily through meditation, rest and play.

Each soul's life is carefully planned before incarnating. Let us picture for a moment the Soul Dimension where you and your soul companions are preparing for the next life on planet Earth. You are deciding on who will play the patient and who will play the doctor. You may argue that you played the patient last time and died from the plague. It is now your turn to be the healer. In the end, you may conclude that you will both be medical doctors in your next lifetime and will bring in some new kind of healing method.

The interaction of the healer and the sick person is part of the divine plan for each and is an excellent example of "good" karma. Many green ray souls thrive on healing and helping others. It raises their own vibrations. It is good work.

Yet, if the soul's purpose is not served by healing, the illness will not be taken away. If the purpose of the disease is to change a person's way of thinking in order to help him move in the direction of the soul's plan for the life, then the illness will continue until that adjustment has been made.

When and only when the individual acknowledges its soul and knows that it is one with God, can it find joy in any experience that comes its way, including illness.

Those who suffer have so many questions. It creates a "Why Zone," like a crown of question marks around the head. Questions are directed to the soul, to the spirit guides, to the angels, to God. We say that each experience adds to your repertoire as a trainee in the School of Creation.

Some people might try to tell you that a illness is a symbol of your lack of spiritual evolvement. This is over-simplification. No one can judge another, because they do not know that soul's plan for the life.

The interaction between healer and patient is an exercise of faith and trust in God. Although many study the physical body, their so-called medicines and cures do not always succeed. Yet, with another healer, a cure may seem miraculous. This interaction is their canvas for creating.

How often we have stressed that this is the goal of all ensouled beings on your planet: merge with your higher self, your soul. Then you bring the light of God into your beautiful world.

Again, we say to you: life on your physical world is a glorious journey. Rejoice in it!

In the journey of life
There are many
Choices.
You are always going
Somewhere!

Chapter Nine

A World of Illusion

What On Earth Are You Creating?

Hotep: *Your world is only an illusion of your making, you know. Each solid thing you see is not what you see. Each person that you know, is not that person. Nothing in your world is real.*

Landi: We beg to differ. It sure feels real to us.

Hotep: *And to you it is very real. Yet, we see you and your world very differently. To us, you are vibrating energy with colored lights flaring out from your bodies, emanating delicious sounds of joyous music. The only thing holding your world together in its illusion is you.*

Landi: Me? How can I do that?

Hotep: *You have been created to do this, to hold your world in your mind, projecting out what you believe and create, keeping it alive with your thoughts and creative efforts.*

What confuses you most often is in trying to keep another's illusion alive when it does not resonate with your visions of "reality." It causes conflict, fear and imbalance. It is like trying to juggle invisible balls in the air. You cannot see where they are going and, therefore, cannot catch them.

With all things, there will be balance. It is the Law of One. Your electromagnetic poles are designed to keep you upon the planet, to keep you from breaking through the veil of illusion and ending the game. Your aura is made up of positive/negative ions that bring balance. Your challenge through this is not just to become balanced but to become neutral or detached.

Souls come to your planet for the privilege of experiencing the electromagnetic energies that create extreme polarities. Neither pole, positive or negative, is better or worse than the other. Your spirit body creates emotions ranging from ecstasy to despair within the human experience. From a soul's perspective, Earth is simply a glorious rol-

lercoaster in some amusement park. It has its extreme ups and downs, chosen as part of the soul's training as a creator.

From the human perspective, these extreme polarities can be painfully uncomfortable at times, while at other times, they can be amazingly joyful. Bringing these extremes into moderation is the key to finding comfort in mind, body and spirit.

When you pull in the slower vibrations of the negative polarity, it creates despair and depression. The energy is heavy and prickly. It destroys laughter and joy, as well as peace and harmony in the life.

The positive polarity brings a wave of flowing energy that is swift and comfortable. It is like swimming with the current, instead of against it. Anytime you find yourself struggling to make things happen, stop and ask if you are creating in the negative polarity. If the answer is "Yes," simply do not continue acting in that manner. Ask for divine guidance to be shown another way that moves you in the current of the positive polarity.

Negative energy is prickly.
Positive energy is smooth.
Balanced energy is joy!

Landi: Why do so many people suffer from depression?

Hotep: *Recurring depression can be the result of a chemical imbalance in the brain. It is sometimes chosen by the soul and its Council of Elders to balance a previous lifetime of extreme negativity. For others, this imbalance is chosen to offer friends, relatives and caregivers an opportunity to express compassion and patience with these individuals.*

Other forms of depression, such as those caused by stress or the feeling of helplessness, offer the opportunity to demonstrate courage and strength through the overcoming of this hurdle. They will be encouraged to develop a sense of humor and kindness, instead of giving into that prickly feeling of anger and impatience.

Yet, we say to you, oftentimes the person suffering from chronic depression may need help from the medical community to ease any form of disharmony within the body, especially with chemical imbalances.

Landi: There are those people who seem to have a trigger temper. Is this also a chemical imbalance?

Hotep: *A person with a trigger temper may seem*

to be "wired" incorrectly. He sees only "doom and gloom," only thinking about what is wrong, instead of rejoicing in what is right. He forgets that what he focuses on will bring to him what he believes to be truth. His mind gets caught in a loop of worry that takes control. This loop pulls him into the negative polarity and locks him there with anger spilling out all over everyone. He is like a beginner soul.

We bless the gift of anger. It is called the "Action Emotion," and is one of your body's early warning systems that all is not right with your soul. It calls the individual to seek balance within. Relief from anger and worry can only come when the person exercises release, forgiving others and self as he lets go of imagined grievances.

Remember, your world is an illusion of your mind's creations. Anger can be destructive to the human body when the individual does not act immediately to relieve that burning energy with a resolution of the conflict. "Sleeping on it" is not always the best thing. Of course, resolving a conflict through violence is never a good idea.

Fear that one's needs may not be met can create anger within the body, mind and spirit. It is felt as a jab of pain in the abdomen or as pressure in the temples or a restriction in the throat or heaviness in the chest. Peaceful communication of your needs can eliminate the buildup of anger. It can be simply a statement that says, "I'm not comfortable with that idea," opening the door to explain what would make you comfortable.

Sometimes it is impossible to change another's point of view or to change a situation in order to achieve your comfort zone. No one can make you feel what you do not choose to feel. Likewise, you cannot make another respond as you desire him to do. A soul's challenge in life may be just to learn this lesson of letting people be exactly who they are!

Speaking your needs in the moment that anger is felt is essential to keeping balance within the body. Yet, it is vitally important to speak with kindness and a firm position of your beliefs. This is not an open invitation to criticize or complain about another's actions. Each person is seeking his own comfort zone. You cannot put expectations on another to leave this comfort zone to create one for you. It is your responsibility to take care of your own needs as much as possible.

The element of release is a practiced virtue, like all the other elements of creation. By recognizing when to act and when to remain still, when to speak and when to remain silent, you have exercised the element of release. Anger can motivate one to act imprudently and without thought of consequences. The art of release tells you when to respond to a situation. It tells you to turn it over to God and the angels and to let go. If you have done everything possible to make a change for your comfort and still there is no change, then it is time to either turn and leave or ignore the situation.

Landi: Do you have any suggestions, Hotep, to help chronic worriers?

Hotep: *Worry? A terrible waste of energy! It is like saying that we do not do our job! Do not forget that you have a Council of Elders, angels and many others in the Spirit Dimension who are ready to serve, council and support you on your journey. Do not forget to call on us! And then—do forget the worry.*

Worry demonstrates a lack of faith and trust in God. You fear that your needs or those of a loved one will not be met. You fear accidents, thieves in the night and other unknown or unexpected negative events to zap you around the next corner. Because you hear and see mostly the disasters of life in the media that focus on negativity and violence, you do not fill the mind with joy, peace and harmony. We encourage awareness of what goes on in your world of illusion, without focusing on violence.

We would suggest that worry is like a wet blanket surrounding you on a cold winter's day. When you send worry energy to another, you send heavy energy that will pull him down. We know this is not your intent. But your thoughts of worry do just that. Instead, we suggest that you mentally send a symbolic image of love, such as a rainbow, a bouquet of flowers, a hug or whatever else you are inspired to do. This will lift up the person rather than pull him down.

For everyday concerns, we will give a visualization to relieve worry. When you have a problem, imagine you are bouncing your ideas for a solution around on a basketball court. When you run out of ideas, stop. Literally holding that imagined basketball in your hands, watch it turn into a glowing ball of light containing your source of worry. Look up to see a hoop held by two angels high above you. Using your hands, throw the ball into the hoop. The angels will catch it. You can't miss. This is symbolic of letting go and giving permission for your angels and God to take over.

There's nothing created within the universe

without first a thought or an idea. What you think becomes your reality. Therefore, it would be well for humans to put a guard on their thoughts, allowing only the fruitful, productive ones to remain, while blessing, releasing and ignoring any others.

Thoughts Become Reality.

If five people pay you a compliment and one a criticism, most will dwell upon that negative comment, pushing away the good ones. We suggest that you reverse that—concentrate on the compliments and blend them into your awareness of self. Take the criticism only as a suggestion for improvement. If it doesn't serve you, eliminate that thought—and perhaps that person, if he does not seek your highest good.

Meditate also on all that we have revealed in this book and know that you really are divinely guided. You cannot fall off the planet without an army of angels catching you and carrying you to the dimension of light and joy.

When you direct your energy from your heart center outward, giving love, consolation, peace and harmony in any situation, you can switch your thinking—and your outcome—from negative to positive.

An act of will
Can switch your
Anxiety
Into a smile.

We have another suggestion to eliminate worry. Create an image of your concern being coated with a healing pink antacid. Think of it as a soothing balm melting into the people concerned, taking care of their indigestion of misunderstanding. While you're at it, coat the planet as well and all the people on it. Then everything will be "in the pink," will it not?

Landi: And everyone can let out a giant belch of relief, right?

Hotep: *Right! As you paint your world pink, do so with a loving, full heart, asking that all needs be met without the necessity to destroy or take from another. This is what you are being called upon to do. As you send out your vision of how you choose* *your life to be—how you choose your world to be—you have already put into motion the fruits of your thoughts. And so, that which you experience in your imagination, you will create and experience in your world of illusion.*

We cannot say this enough or with enough emphasis. . .

YOU
ARE
CREATORS!

And as you think, so shall you be. How many wise men and women have taught this in so many different ways? It is truth. That's why it comes in so many different forms. We will say it as many times as it needs to be said to help you understand that unless you allow joy and sunshine to enter your life, you will have a sad life, for you have not made room for the joyous light of God.

We have seen your big, yellow smiley face that is commonly used. We suggest that you project this picture into your thoughts as a reminder to laugh. The laughing face will change your negative vibration into a positive one. Vibrations are constantly changing all around you. You live in a world of illusion of your own making. It is your canvas for creating whatever you desire to experience.

Create Through Joy!

Since you are a co-creator with God, you must realize that you cannot create anything of value without first entering into the presence of that One that is Joy. When you lift your vibrations into that space of love, you cannot help but create beauty and goodness in your life.

Landi: But, Hotep, our world is not all "love and light." How can we create through joy when we rarely feel it?

Hotep: *Joy comes through practice, through deliberately seeking it, through a strong determination to experience it. We strongly recommend daily relaxation and meditation for everyone. We also recommend laughter and play. We remind you that you are not alone. God has not abandoned you on this planet that seems to have much* *sadness and despair. Indeed, you have angels and guides and a whole cheering section of helpers who seek only good for you.*

Rejoice and be glad in all things, giving praise and thanks to God who is the Creator of All.

Landi: Finances can become another source of great worry for people. What can they do about it?

Hotep: *Many people fall into depression and worry because of the helpless feeling that they cannot control their lives. Some have created tremendous debts by resorting to the use of credit cards to "tide them over" until the next paycheck.*

We encourage you to limit credit cards to only the amount you can pay off each month. The interest accumulated is like paying the loan sharks of old—making them rich and keeping you in debt until you are lost in despair.

The need for "instant gratification" of acquiring "things" of pleasure and comfort begins the downward spiral into debt and despair. One cannot buy today and pay tomorrow without the consequences of debt. Waiting for the money to purchase the desired object creates discipline and patience, which are gems of wisdom for the soul.

We suggest that people use a check register to itemize the purchases with credit cards, for without a written ledger of totals, most will over-spend. For some, it would be wise to give up the temptation of credit cards altogether. Too often, the misuse of them has caused bankruptcy. This is not "good work." Leaving a debt unpaid creates an imbalance that must be settled at a future time. We encourage you to be frugal but not "tight" with your money. We also encourage you to put aside a percentage of your income for the future.

Landi: With people struggling to make ends meet, how can anyone save money for that "rainy day?"

Hotep: *Unfortunately, your financial institutions make debt too appealing, such that people expect to owe banks for houses and cars. "No money down" is a lure of irresponsible actions that will lead to stress and depression when the light of reality dawns.*

Saving for that dream home, that dream car, advanced education or a well-deserved vacation is a worthy goal. But one must also put aside a cushion for the unexpected breakdown of appliances or automobiles that require maintenance. Saving for these kinds of things is a wise and pru-

dent use of finances.

Saving For a future expenditure Is the only way to Avoid debt.

We have suggested to many that keeping their finances recorded on a computer program will eliminate the guesswork in their financial situation. In a family, especially, it is imperative that both partners and older children be informed of the family budget. Too often, the head of the family will not wish to share that information out of fear that he might lose control or that certain members will overspend. This again is an opportunity for spiritual growth. A budget is always necessary to remain solvent in your ever-changing world.

Bankruptcy is a red flag for the soul. Any debt that is not paid means future lives of paying debts. There is no escape from the responsibility of your actions. There may, of course, be exceptions, such as astronomical medical bills that would be impossible to pay off in one lifetime. These are social issues that need to be addressed by those who govern your society.

Money is a form of energy exchange. Think of money this way and you will eliminate much confusion. For example, those who serve others need to have some form of recompense for that service. This is not to be confused with true charity where one gives without thought of return. Yet, it is another element of creation that says, "You cannot give to another without giving to self." That gift may be a return of generosity that had been given to you previously. This is an example of "good karma."

Landi: What about tithing? Churches say that we need to give 10% of our income back to God.

Hotep: *God has no need of money. The church does. You have a need to be of service to others. Your "tithing" can be in that venue. We discourage anyone from giving either time or money if they feel pressured to do so. If the gift is not freely given with joy in the heart, it will not gain the person or his soul the benefits.*

Always check your motivations for giving to another. For example: if you give so others can see that you have given, you have lost the gift of generosity for your soul.

Beware of giving to another when your own family needs it for basic sustenance. Many people have the belief that if they give a percentage of their income back to God, they will have increased income to spend as they desire. This motivation in itself defeats the purpose of charity. The reward of increased income is what you seek, rather than the desire to serve others. Always search your heart for your intent before you tithe or give to a charity. Also, be aware of the guilt strings that can be strummed by others to get into your pocketbook.

The lessons learned from the management of finances gains the human and the soul great spiritual advancement and wisdom. Do not perceive the experience lightly.

Landi: The loss of a job can cause great stress because bills have to be paid. If there is no money coming in, what can a person do?

Hotep: *Career changes are often created by the soul to move the entity into another path for greater opportunities of soul advancement. Although losing a job is most stressful, an open mind filled with trust will move the person into another source of income more quickly. As always, fear* *slams the door to any help from your guides who can make this transition smooth and rewarding. A joyous heart allows us to bring together those people who can provide the source of new income.*

When you find yourself surrounded by chaos and stress within your world of illusion, you do feel like the salmon swimming upstream. That is the time to find a quiet place, close your eyes and take a few moments to breathe deeply. Go within and imagine yourself in your favorite chair placed in sunshine amidst a beautiful scene in nature. Breathe in the flowers that surround you. Feel the warmth of the sun on your face. Feel your entire body filling up with peace and joy. Give grateful thanks for this moment in time. Then open your eyes and continue your day.

Daily meditation is an essential ingredient for balancing the body, mind, emotions and spirit. As each human brings these elements into alignment, their life flows more smoothly.

Daily laughter speeds that smooth alignment. It is the elixir of the soul, helping you adjust to the many changes in your life.

And change is a given ingredient in the creative process. You are never the same as you were a moment ago. Yet, we say to you that as long as you are in the physical, you will bounce from one polarity to the other. You will feel sad; you will feel happy. You will experience worry; you will experience peace. You will know loss and pain; you will know abundance and joy. It is part of the human condition. You cannot change that but your free will allows you to choose how you will react in any given situation. That becomes your world. Change gives you the gift of creating balance. If you don't like what you see, change your viewpoint and create anew!

Change begins within your mind. It receives information through that wondrous mechanism called a brain. The right lobe of the brain is your connection with us. It takes in all of your surroundings through your five senses without labeling or judging them. It then sends that information to the left side of your brain that categorizes, labels and judges same as "good" or "bad" according to previous experiences. All of this is instantly recorded by your soul, sometimes called the "super-conscious mind."

Obviously, fears color your conscious mind's judgment and, therefore, is not very reliable. Do not trust it! Always take your information into your super-conscious mind before making any major decisions.

All your fears are stored in the subcon-

scious mind, called your "emotional body." It is without reason or knowledge. It only feels. Treat it like your inner child, with reassurance that it is not alone, that it has not been abandoned. Recognize your fears as an expression of unresolved issues. By speaking to your subconscious mind in deep meditation, you resolve those issues and free yourself from future pain.

Always think of yourself as "We," just as we do. When we speak in the plural, we are recognizing our connection with everyone and everything in the universe as God. There are a lot of "We's" around you, are there not?

Landi: Yes, there are. Next time when I'm feeling very alone, I'll remember that three makes a crowd. I can talk to "me," my conscious mind; "myself," my subconscious mind; and "I" as my soul. "We" shall be best friends.

Hotep: *Good! Knowing that you are not alone in your world of illusion can bring you joy. Fear creates a cloud cover so thick that you shut us out, making it impossible for us to send you the smiley face of laughter.*

Landi: Hotep, you always seem so incredibly

happy and filled with laughter. How can we be more like you?

Hotep: *Heaven forbid! Is not one Hotep enough for the universe?*

Yes, you feel our joy because we are one with God. This is why we urge you to become one with your soul. It's the first step in becoming Joy.

And so, now we will speak of laughter! It is a good thing. You can never have enough of it. We say to you: there is joy in all of life, even the seemingly scary experiences. Laughter creates joy. It is so necessary for people to develop a funny bone. Many have these somber bones which make them see life through a tunnel vision of doom and gloom. Oh my! They do bring in the negativity. They do not even know that they do this. Doom and gloom are all they can see and so they expect it like a rainy day.

In actuality, by allowing joy to enter in, you raise your vibrations so that you can cooperate with Mother Nature and create the sunshine. But even when the clouds bring rain, create your own sunshine through laughter and joy. This is the most important thing for soul growth that exists—laughter! You can advance more quickly with a sense of humor and with the idea that you are God.

The Creator is joy and laughter and love and that's all It is. When you tap into God, that's where you are—in the Joy that embraces and enfolds you, giving the comfort and love that you so dearly seek.

Many begin their search for joy in their physical world. They look and look but cannot find it. Next, they seek it in someone else's world and are again disappointed. This is often because they are expecting only doom and gloom.

To find joy, you must create it. Do something every day to make yourself laugh. If you don't create laughter within yourself, you starve your soul of God's nourishment. Laughter opens up the gateways by which you can receive knowledge from God, helping you do the things that you need to do; that you desire in your heart to do. These desires are put there by God for good—not for manipulating other people to get your needs taken care of, whether sexually, physically, or to fill your belly. No! No! No! God desires only to create something fruitful and good .

Laughter
Is the
Sweet nectar
Of life.

And so we say to you: each day do something to bring laughter into your world. If you must, go out and buy the laughter book; those you call joke books, yes? Have one beside the toilet, because when you are eliminating, it is symbolic of eliminating all of this doom and gloom, while the laughter is filling you up, you see. So put one in every bathroom.

Landi: So instead of the proverbial, "A chicken in every stewing pot," you're saying to have a "Joke book beside every 'chamber pot.'"

Hotep: *Yes! This is good!*

Another thing: Never take yourself too seriously. We cannot emphasize this enough. And so each day on your agenda, make a time for laughter—by telling a joke on yourself. When you do the foolish things, like putting the milk on the shelf and the cereal in the refrigerator, tell someone about it. Laugh at self!

What happened to the days of sitting around the campfire and telling funning stories? Nobody takes time to do this anymore. We say: do it again.

And so, first and most importantly, begin this day by laughing at your world of illusion. And each person who reads these words— find something funny about your perspective of the world to tell another. Be the comedian. Brighten their day and yours, too.

When little things happen that cause you to laugh, stop and listen to the wisdom that comes with that, for there is always a purpose. Laughing at one's self every day means that you are overcoming self. Further, when you worry about what others will think of you, you are caught in a downward spiral and you will end up doing things that will create embarrassment. Out of fear, you will trip over your own feet, say the wrong thing, even belch—in front of everyone! And there you are—stuck! Nothing can be done then but laugh.

We tell you that all of your guides are helping you to laugh at self. Some of you experience life with such pain because of your fear of being ridiculed or hurt by the silliness of the human condition. The human body is silly to begin with. It is made mostly of water and it sloshes around!

Remember to fill each day with laughter. Search for the funny parts of it by looking at life from a higher perspective. True, there are inexperienced souls that may have trouble doing this but we know that if they are taught how to do it—if they are brought into the awareness— they shall succeed.

Become aware of your thoughts. The moment you hear words of self-deprecation, stop and laugh at yourself. The moment you feel the numbness that comes when you're so afraid that someone may hurt you, choose to laugh at it instead. In so doing, you create a different perspective, a different attitude. This will create a different world.

Landi: Can laughter literally create sunshine when it's pouring rain outside?

Hotep: *This is possible, however, most people on your planet are not evolved enough to do this. Laughter cannot bring the sunshine except in your heart.*

Yet, you are always creating with your thoughts projecting your mind into those rain clouds. You can begin to break them up. See yourself as spirit whooshing at the clouds, making them blow away or as an airplane zooming through the clouds and letting the sun come through. When you visualize and image it, using a powerful act of will, then it becomes so; it is done, for you have created it.

Landi: It would be great if we could eliminate pain by imagining it away.

Hotep: *And why would it not be the same with fear and pain? Choose to create a perspective of humor, therein opening your mind to receive a solution to relieve that situation. In so doing, you create an atmosphere for helping the fear to disappear and the pain to become tolerable.*

For most people, life is this push-me, pull-me struggle, trying to get the most out of it in order to survive. Many do not understand that creating through fear brings the rain into their lives, whereas creating through joy and laughter brings the sunshine. This is the key to being co-creators with God, which supplies the energy for all that they need.

Landi: In other words, always think positive thoughts.

Hotep: *No. When people believe that they must only think positive, uplifting thoughts every moment of every day, they can become trapped under the illusion of "rose-colored glasses." This may be demonstrated in refusing to look at anything as a problem, thereby ignoring opportunities for growth. It can also be seen in the extreme through inappropriate euphoria, such as silliness or giddy behavior. Those who will interrupt another's serious conversation to tell an inappropriate joke or laugh at someone's misfortune, are demonstrating immature soul qualities of the positive polarity.*

At the present time on your world, more and more souls are coming closer to a comfortable and more balanced vibration in the middle of these extremes. Most do not go all the way into either polarity as they did in the past—yet some will continue to do this.

When you know that there is a higher purpose for everything that happens, whether good or bad, you will begin to see the humor in it and will begin to experience more and more joy.

We are done. Blessings of laughter upon you.

A Balanced

Earth

Chapter Ten

A Balanced Earth

Predictions of the Future

Landi: I'm concerned about the future of our planet, Raphael. Can you tell us what will happen to Earth regarding ecological changes, weather and the like?

Raphael: *Your planet is overseen by a very large old soul that we shall call "Mother Earth." She has progressed beyond the physical creation of matter within the dense atmosphere of the positive/negative energy where she may have created a chair, so to speak. She has now graduated to the point of creating a planet.*

Advancement has to do with the individual soul's ability to be as an arm of the Creator, God.

The more you advance into the knowledge that you are One with God, the more you can gain access to the creative process. Yes, that advanced soul, Mother Earth, has created your planet. She is ensouled in the planet, just as your soul is ensouled within you.

Landi: Then who oversees Mother Earth's soul?

Raphael: *While Mother Earth is the overseer of her planet, she also has a Council of Elders who have had experience in creating planets. They guide and help her in her creation. Mother Earth has been learning how to work with her body's inhabitants and all of the physics of human and earth nature. Now she is ready to move to a higher level of her education where she desires to bring her energy to a point that her creation, Earth, can more easily heal itself. In her long-ago physical incarnations, she learned the art of healing physical bodies. She now must learn the art of healing her planetary body as she cooperates with ensouled humans dwelling upon her planet.*

As an example, Mother Earth might send the message to humans to help her stop the destruction of her rain forests. She might reveal that her body will not survive without the moisture that it needs to replenish itself. She will inspire as many human minds as she can to save that part of her, obtaining in this cooperation a better understanding that she is one with all these humans running around her planet like ants. Mother Earth has spirit helpers and angels, as well as a Council, just as you do. She is at a much higher vibration than what you need to exist at this particular time.

To help you understand Mother Earth's dilemma with her creation, let us use the analogy of her being the CEO of her own company, her brainchild, Earth. She has nurtured and helped this company to grow. She has employed certain people to play certain roles to bring her ideas into physicality.

Now, suppose that in the first two years she finds that there are those within the organization who are stealing from her precious company. When she finds this out, she fires them. She gets rid of them. Now, let us take this on a global view. Suppose that on your particular planet there were those who figured out how to tap into the resources of Mother Earth and were stealing them for their own personal gain. She might tolerate it at first and watch, knowing that these are beginner souls who do not know any better. Finally, after allowing those physical life-extensions to end and go back into the Spirit Dimension, she would not want those souls to return. Mother Earth might go to the Soul Dimension and give a lecture to those who had enjoyed her planet, telling them that her planet needs to be honored and nurtured so that they can continue to come and enjoy it. If they do not, then she will not allow them to return.

But suppose, like a child ignoring his mother's warning of dire consequences, these souls continued to incarnate in human form on Mother Earth, forgetting their purpose to help her and forgetting to give praise to God for the pleasures of her body.

Mother Earth watched and waited but to no avail. Thus she went to a higher authority, to her Council of Elders and made certain that those souls were no longer allowed to incarnate upon her planet.

Landi: Did this happen to some civilizations a long time ago?

Raphael: *Yes, it did. Some civilizations were eliminated and for a time, long ago, beginner souls were denied access to this planet—as they will be again, if they continue to create humans who bring havoc and destruction. The planet must be free of* *interference and have time to heal itself again. She asked that more advanced souls be sent to help heal and restore her body.*

Landi: Where did the souls come from that were called in to help Mother Earth?

Raphael: *Some of the advanced souls were called from other planets and from other dimensions. Some took on human form when they were needed to help evolve a species as they are now doing. These souls came from many places, "to raise the consciousness," as you would say. In the present times, the DNA of the more advanced souls newly incarnating will be more in tune with the Spirit and Soul Dimensions.*

Landi: I've always been curious, Raphael. How did we end up with so many different races?

Raphael: *Let us again use the example of Mother Earth as the CEO of a very large company. When she first began to form the planet, she called many advanced souls who had finished incarnations on other systems. They came as scientists, ecologists and gardeners to help seed her planet with various life-forms. Because these employees/souls created* *vehicles for ensoulment, their human vehicles had features that resembled their own soul's previous body forms from their planetary systems. They adapted them so that they would survive in the varying climates on Earth. Some of these human vehicles did not survive but several diverse races did, thus creating a variety of color and body types.*

You are Children Of the Stars.

Landi: You mean that just like the U.S. is called the "melting pot of nations," the whole planet is a melting pot of other planetary beings?

Raphael: *Yes. Most of you have hereditary genetics from beings that you call extraterrestrials.*

Now, just as a soul progresses through its various stages of incarnation as a human being, so, too, has Mother Earth. Her planet has moved through its different stages of growth and she has gained the understanding of how various life forms survive or perish. Earth has evolved over millions of years. Yet linear time is but a blink of the eye for the large soul called Mother Earth. She is gaining great wisdom through her precious blue jewel in the universe. Rejoice in that. Speak to the soul of Mother Earth. Rejoice in her beauty and bless her in work well done.

Landi: Raphael, what ever happened with the census that Hotep and all the Councils were taking? Has it been completed?

Raphael: *Yes it has. We say: Be at peace and rejoice in the coming of a balanced Earth. Yes, that is what the completion of the census means. Mother Earth asked—no demanded—that this census be taken of all ensouled beings manifesting upon her evolving body now and in the future.*

Landi: You sound very excited about it. This is good news then?

Raphael: *It is indeed good news for all in the Universe. With the gathering of all the Councils who created the census, souls came before them to state their intent for future incarnations on Earth. They had to account for any destruction their human vehicles had created and then explain how and when they would rectify that damage. Those souls who desired to complete their incarnational* *cycle on Earth had to agree to choose more balanced entities who would work for the greater good of all mankind and not for the individual's wealth and power.*

For some souls, this was a very difficult decision. Their Councils recognized that their human creations must reap what they had sown in that they would experience the bad and the good they had previously created. For example, some humans have gathered great wealth at the expense of the planet's natural resources. Where one called Tesla had discovered how to harness electricity for the free use of all, another, that we will not name, prevented this discovery and used it for his own gain. Hence greed caused people to have to pay for electricity ever since. Other inventions have been squelched throughout your history, such as most recently, an automobile that would run one hundred miles per gallon of gasoline. Those who sought their own selfish gain buried that invention, as well as many wonderful creations that others had worked on while in the Spirit Dimension.

These selfish acts disappointed that human's soul who knew that the balance would require an unpleasant experience in the future. Perhaps their human might experience an invention that is taken from him. He would clamor loudly at the "injustice," yet it would be but a balance for a previous act of like kind.

Please note: not all unjust acts are the result of a previous act of injustice. It is not that simple. Do not listen to anyone who would suggest it is so.

Remember that it is the soul's judgment that creates a belief as truth in its educational process. When the souls came before their Council of Elders for this census, nothing could be hidden. Each soul had to account for everything. Blessed are those who are exhibiting integrity and kindness to others and to the planet. They will know peace in their next incarnation.

Nothing is hidden.
Every act,
Both "good" and "bad,"
Requires balancing.

This refers to the elements of God, to that divine Law of Love that is always working in each life. Masters on your planet have acknowledged the cause of fortune and misfortune in one's life and encouraged the multitudes to seek goodness and justice in their world. These Masters from every race—and from the stars—have become one with God in the Law of Love and speak truth as truth. It would do well for all to listen to them.

And so this census that took many of your earth years to complete will spin itself out with this generation of inhabitants upon the planet. When the body dies, the spirit entity will go to the Spirit Dimension and complete its cycle for that life. The soul will meet again with its Council of Elders and plan the next life. It is then that the choice will be evident.

The next generation of humans will be more enlightened and aware of their oneness with God. You have seen this with younger children already on the planet. Some call them the "Indigo children." Others call them "Star Seeds." As you remember, the indigo soul color is a much higher vibration than most of the beginner souls from the red ray that have dominated the material world for so long.

Landi: Some would call those souls who come through the red ray 'warrior souls.' If they were of the beginner soul age, that would account for the many wars and fighting that has been plaguing the planet for centuries. Are you saying that this is going to change? Are there going to be less warrior souls on earth?

Raphael: *Not necessarily. Your red-ray souls are excellent leaders and will be greatly needed in the years to come to reorganize and rebuild the planet's natural resources. Already there are many working on this.*

Landi: How will our resources be 'rebuilt?' Is it even possible if we have depleted them?

Raphael: *For some it is not possible. You have made many of Mother Earth's creatures extinct due to overpopulation and greed for water, land and other valuable resources. In the coming times, the human population will thin, as it already is doing through natural disasters, illness and wars.*

Mother Earth will have balance. Just as her forests can burn seemingly out of control and then over time rebuild to be healthier than before, so, too, can she recover other resources or reinvent new ones. Remember, Mother Earth has called in her "troops" of advanced souls who can create new life upon the planet when she will have a time of peace to do so.

All souls who will have the privilege of incarnating upon Mother Earth's body in the future will have to dedicate their efforts to healing her. As previously stated, you will see this manifesting within the next fifty to one-hundred years.

We are well aware of skeptics regarding any predictions of future events. We concur—the future is always flexible because you are creating it. It is not our purpose to persuade or convince anyone of what we say. It is always our purpose to bring God's love, light and peace to your planet.

You can choose to have a future that is wonderful, peaceful and joyous. Although the planet and many of its people will still experience trials, tribulations and tumultuous upheavals during this transition, you can create a safe haven as you merge with your soul and follow its guidance.

We call upon all of those who read this book to become actively involved in solving Mother Earth's needs, until we are certain that her precious blue jewel is safe and sound and joyously moving into her new glorified body.

Landi: What does that mean—her "glorified body?"

Raphael: *It means that when she is able to regain her health and begin to allow her beautiful energy to shine, she will glow so brightly that the whole universe will be aware of her beauty. Many souls will come to see how this planet has not only recovered but has become one of the leaders in planetary development. You have every right to bless and be proud of your little globe. It shall become a star in the universal drama.*

Earth's aura
Shall glow like a star
In the universal drama.

Again, we remind you that this process of change for planet Earth and all of humanity is ongoing. There will be great changes in the interaction between souls as well. Their once comfortable soul family or soul group, where they "grew up together," can be split up, with some moving foreword while others will be left behind. This is the way of soul development even now. Some souls catch on to the art of creating quicker than others.

As we have said, it will take approximately fifty to one-hundred of your years for the mass consciousness of humans to balance, thus lessening the wars and prejudices on your planet.

Mother Earth is calling upon awakened souls to assist in this ongoing endeavor through group action to heal her planet. Her soul may inspire people to write articles or to lecture on ecology and recycling or to pray and meditate about the healing of her beloved Earth. All over the globe, lights are turning on as humans awaken to her call. It is like a Christmas tree. Delightful!

One of these changes has manifested as the thinning of the veil between dimensions. People are beginning to communicate with spirits on the other side. For some, the first occurrence will frighten them. However, it gives them the opportunity to take a second look at themselves and their beliefs. More people are beginning to awaken and are eager to learn the truth about spirit, about God. If this continues to happen, your species will gain great wisdom, thus experiencing peace in the years to come.

Another factor bringing balance to your planet is that souls incarnate with an already expanded awareness or as you might say, an "upgraded DNA." They are writing books that are flying off the shelves, quenching the thirst of those desiring knowledge about the other side.

Still more advanced souls, who are from

other planetary systems in your universe, have agreed to take on human form at this particular time during your transition. They will manifest ideas and suggestions from their Council of Elders on how to heal Mother Earth. They will also be instrumental in becoming a bridge of tolerance between humans and nations of your world and between species and nations of other worlds.

Because of the delicate balance of this transition, we have even sent angelic beings to become ensouled in human form. They anchor the light of God's unconditional love within your dimension and your planet.

All of you are working to bring balance to Mother Earth as she evolves, choosing to serve the planet and one another, as God.

As the shift in consciousness occurs, much of the negativity will come to the surface—to be seen by everyone—and will seem to dominate. But the exposure to the Light of God will weaken this trend toward destruction and greed and, indeed, it will dissipate, creating the balance that is needed on your planet.

Because your thought patterns are ever changing, we can never say for sure about anything in the future; however, we can tell you that your planet is going to change drastically in its weather conditions. This is necessary for balance. What you have already set into motion with your wars and disruption to the Earth's magnetic poles and atmosphere, will have to be endured.

Mass thought patterns
Determine
What you will
Create for your
Future.

Landi: That concurs with visions that I've been shown where there will be chaos and war and food supplies may be disrupted. I was told that garden implements may become more valuable than gold.

Raphael*:* *The truth of God's love is always manifesting through your seeming disasters. You have already seen what can happen when the eastern United States was suddenly without electricity. Yet one of the good things that came from that was the drastic drop in air pollution.*

It is also a clear message how easily your physical world of illusion can change. Your physical world is subject to the laws of the Physical Di-

mension. For example, natural resources will diminish as population grows. "Brownouts" and power outages will increase. Therefore, it would be wise and responsible to prepare for unexpected changes by keeping a storage of supplies, such as food and water.

Mother Earth will have balance—no matter what. Humans will reap what they have sown in the stripping of her natural resources, in irresponsible procreation and in the devastation brought about by greed, power and wars.

Most humans are so steeped in their physical comforts that they are not prepared for any loss of electricity or food. Yet, times may come when those garden implements may be worth their weight in gold as you have seen.

We suggest that each person prepare as though the worst-case scenario might happen and pray that the minds and hearts of nations will change the vision's outcome.

And yet, we say to you, beloved souls: this is a joyous process. All planets shift and change. Any scientist will tell you that Earth's currents, from the airways to the oceans, are constantly changing.

Landi: There have been those who have predicted

that a planet is going to pass close to Earth sometime in the not-so-distant future. Wouldn't that cause great havoc on the planet?

Raphael *On a global scale, Earth is experiencing its own cause and effect, not exclusively from what people do to it. Because of its natural evolution, the universe is always going through cycles, as in birth and death. Change is a given. And so the planet is going through its evolutionary cycle of growth, which is generally very, very slow. However, when this other planet passes by, the waves will create the changes to happen much faster. The fear that most humans have is that they may be caught in that change and be frozen on the spot.*

Landi: As in another ice age?

Raphael: *The coming changes will not be as drastic as an ice age. Yet we remind you that you are spirit and spirit rejoices in change. The soul knows what is coming—to a certain extent. However, even though your soul sees a bigger picture, it does not have all knowingness, nor do we as Raphael, nor does Hotep. No one does, except God, who is the mechanism by which the universe* *cycles and moves. It is part of your education to learn to trust God. Planetary changes might cause many human bodies to exit but remember, your soul lives on. Therefore, there is nothing to fear.*

REJOICE!
You are safe.
Your planet is just
Stretching.

Do not forget that your planet, Earth, has a soul. And as an ensouled being, it would not leave its future in the hands of fearful human occupants. It has called upon God in its time of change to send souls that are Masters in the ways of planetary evolution. This shift that we are talking about has been slowed by the efforts of many ensouled beings with their prayers and thoughts of healing. There are spirit, soul and angelic energies that have put a vibrational grid around your Earth to keep the waves of the passing planet from shifting your world too abruptly. Mother Earth herself is working to make the shift easier in her rotation around the sun. The planet will shift less than predicted but can indeed change the polarities. And that in itself would cause a lot of problems.

The shift, for example, with all of its glacier activity at the poles, has been creating a warming of your atmosphere. Huge chunks of ice fall into the ocean, which in turn changes the weather patterns of those large bodies of water. These Earth changes will probably take one to two thousand years to complete.

Landi: Was there a drastic pole shift on this planet in the past?

Raphael: *Yes. The last ice age froze all of your different life forms.*

Landi: Since you say that the present shift is happening in increments, will we be warned with enough time to leave endangered areas?

Raphael: *We do not mean to frighten you, to make people want to run this way or that way to avoid these changes. We say to you again that when you choose the joy and inner peace that merges with the energy of God, you will become aware of your divine guidance. It is your soul speaking to you. Then you can let go of your fear of being in the wrong place at the wrong time. No matter what happens, it will be the right place, if* *that is what your soul chooses to experience. Remember: life changes are a given. They bring the challenges that allow for the development of great courage and strength of character. Learn this early on and you will not fear life's changes.*

Landi: Raphael, is there still a possibility that we might blow our planet into oblivion with our nuclear weapons?

Raphael: *There is always that possibility but that threat has lessened with more global awareness of the consequences.*

The human mind is beginning to open up to a broader spectrum where it can increase its sense of joy and knowingness of God. With that, you can realize your role in creation, accepting full responsibility for the consequences of that knowledge. You, individually and as a species, are totally responsible for what you do on your planet. As the human race accepts this truth, Mother Earth will be healed. And it is good.

We say to you so often: rejoice and be glad for the awareness of the universal love that is God within you creating within this planet. Compared to the magnificence of the universe, you may see yourself as a grain of sand in the ocean. Yet each human is as important to the evolution of your planet, as are all those who create the grid to slow the planet's shift. Add your energies to this project through your daily meditations. Mother Earth will thank you.

We encourage each of you to follow the lighted path of the Divine Laws of Creation in the days to come. We call upon you to follow the inner guidance of your soul in bringing about peace, first within yourself, then within your family and friends and then within your planet.

There are so many now incarnate on your world who heed the urgent message to bring about peaceful change for your globe. Many feel the need for action but cannot discern what to do about it or where they fit in the bigger picture.

What you can do is first merge with your own soul, your divinity, allowing its light to shine brightly in each moment of your life. Project to others compassion, love, tolerance, peace and joy. In that, you will change your planet into a heaven on Earth. It shall become a reality when you hold fast to the vision that it is so.

The vision is the key.

Do not hold on to a fear of disaster or you shall create that instead. Indeed, many have already done this. No. Hold fast to the vision of the end of wars and the end of that brutal enforcement of one's will over another. Hold fast to the conversion of war machines into implements for peace. Only then will you have an enlightened world.

Remember, each of you is guided by many on this side who continually project their brilliant lights into your world. Be at peace in knowing this. By merging with your soul and God, your task to uplift and rejuvenate your planet will bring peace to your world. This task is not insurmountable. It shall become a reality when you hold fast to that vision of peace and harmony within yourself and your planet.

You have done well, beloved ones. We are always with you. Peace and joy in creating your new world.

We are the World.

We Create a Balanced Earth.

About the Authors

Betty Rae, B.S., M.Ed.

Betty Rae has been a clairvoyant for over fifty years, counseling hundreds of people all across the U.S., Canada and Europe. Her ardent search for God and truth was a precursor to contact with the angelic realm. The unconditional love and non-judgment this contact brings adds to her gentle humor and wisdom. She is an ordained Christian minister honoring all faiths.

As a musician, artist, published author and retired teacher of music and English with a Master's Degree in Education, Betty Rae continues to be involved in counseling people by telephone or in her home that has come to be called, *Angel House*.

In 1997, Under the name of Betty Rae Calleja (she no longer uses her past husband's surname), she published an eight-week course in spiritual development with four guided meditations called *Come, Play with the Angels.* She has also published a channeled work called *Letters from a Guardian Angel* which includes forty of her original pastel drawings.

Always in continual communication with her spirit guides and the Archangel Raphael, Betty Rae is currently working on another channeled book and a novel.

Landi B. Mellas, C.M.P.

Since Landi was seven, she has encountered visits from extraterrestrials. It wasn't until 2002 that this well-kept secret was revealed in the publishing of her book, *The Other Sky*. With her late co-author, David Caywood, they joined the ranks of the multitudes of people who were coming forward with their encounters with ETs.

Landi was featured on the Sci-Fi channel documentary *Abduction Diaries* that aired before Stephen Spielberg's television series, *Taken.* Out of many people interviewed across the country, only six were selected. Her ability to accept her experiences with humor and trust has made her an "Experiencer of the Profound," rather than a "Victim of Alien Abduction." She has found that many of these beings have great wisdom and compassion for the human race.

Because of these "other-worldly" events, Landi began searching for answers early in life, studying with the yogis and becoming a Certified Metaphysical Practitioner. She helps people increase their awareness of spirit guides and otherworldly beings. Many "Experiencers" are sent to Landi by professionals in the field of Ufology to help them see the spiritual viewpoint in their encounters.